Johnny Ball

GO FIGURE!

DK PUBLISHING, INC.

LONDON, NEW YORK, MUNICH,
MELBOURNE, and DELHI

Author Johnny Ball
Senior editor Ben Morgan
Senior art editor Claire Patané
Designer Sadie Thomas
DTP designer Almudena Díaz
Picture researcher Anna Bedewell
Production Emma Hughes

Publishing manager Susan Leonard
Managing art editor Clare Shedden

Consultant Sean McArdle

First American Edition, 2005

Published in the United States by
DK Publishing, Inc.
375 Hudson Street
New York, New York 10014

06 07 08 09 10 9 8 7 6 5 4 3 2

A catalog record for this book
is available from the Library of Congress.

ISBN:13 978-0-7566-1374-7
ISBN:10 0-7566-1374-4

Color reproduction by Icon Reproductions, London
Printed and bound in China by SNP Leefung

Discover more at
www.dk.com

I didn't do all that well in school, but I did love math. When I left school, I found that I still wanted to know more, and math became my lifelong hobby. I love math and all things mathematical.

Everything we do depends on math. We need to count things, measure things, calculate and predict things, describe things, design things, and solve all sorts of problems—and all these things are best done with math.

There are many different branches of math, including some you may never have heard of. So we've tried to include examples and illustrations, puzzles and tricks from almost every different kind of math. Or at least from the ones we know about—someone may have invented a completely new kind while I was writing this introduction.

So come and meander through the weird and wonderful world of math—I'm sure there will be lots of things that interest you, from magic tricks and mazes to things you can do and make. To get you started, just think of a number. The thought could take you anywhere....

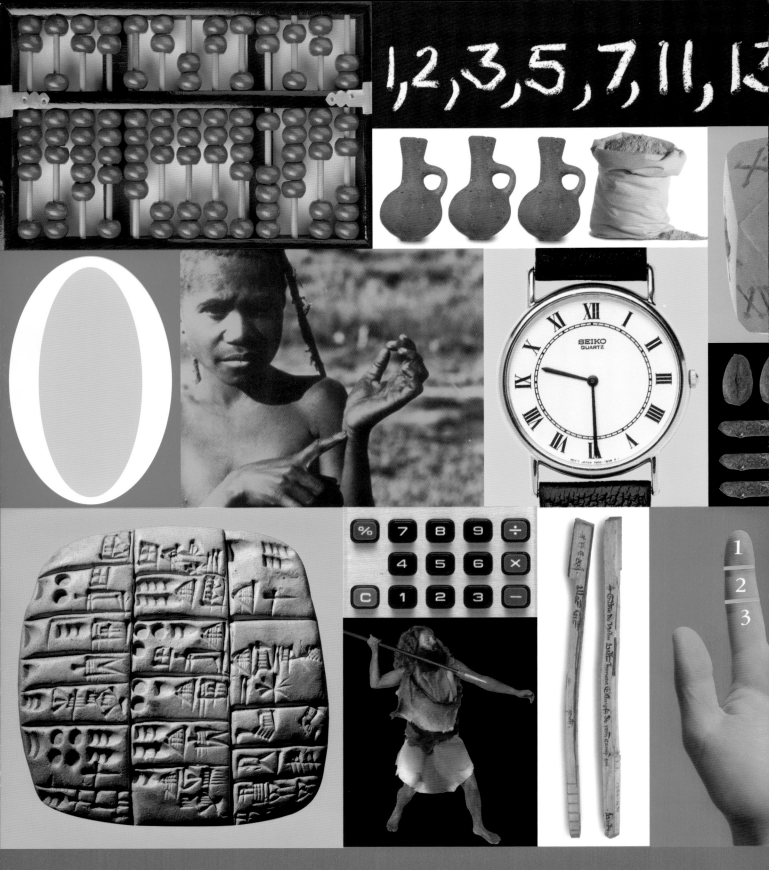

1, 2, 3, 5, 7, 11, 13

Where do **NUMBERS** come from?

"Numbers help us in so many ways. We don't just count with them, we count on them. Without numbers we wouldn't know the time or date. We wouldn't be able to buy things, count how many things we have, or complain about how many things we don't have.

So numbers had to be invented. The story of their invention is full of fascinating twists and turns, and it took people a long time to hit on the simple system we use today.

Now numbers are everywhere and we need them for everything. Just imagine what the world would be like if we didn't have numbers..."

Price
●●●●●●●●●●
this many coins

WORLD

Huge crowd wins lottery

Jack Potter

The winning balls for Saturday's national lottery were red, red, blue, yellow, yellow, and white.

A huge crowd of jackpot winners arrived at lottery headquarters on Sunday to claim the prize, forming a line that stretched all the way across town.

The total prize fund is currently several housefuls of money. The fund will be handed out in cupfuls until all the money is gone.

Sheeza Wonnalot was among the lucky jackpot winners.

Woman has some babies

A woman in India has given birth to lots of babies at once.

The babies are all about the size of a small pineapple, and doctors say they are doing very well.

Sally Armstrong

Although it's common for a woman to give birth to a baby and another, and there are sometimes cases of

a woman giving birth to a baby and another and another, this woman gave birth to a baby and another and another and another and another and another.

Soccer team scores

NEWS

Full TV Listings *on the page before the page before the page before the last page*

World Weather

by Windy Gusts

London		Sunny but not especially warm	**Rio**		Really sweltering, drink lots of water
Paris		Rainy and cold enough for coats	**Delhi**		Wet and warm but not too warm
New York		Hot enough for T-shirts	**Sydney**		Cold and cloudy— long-sleeves weather
Munich		Freezing cold— wear a warm hat	**Tokyo**		Lots of rain expected, take your umbrella

Gold medals went to Ima Springyleg and Harry Foot.

lots and lots of goals

Johnny Ball

England won the soccer World Cup yet another time yesterday when they beat Brazil by several goals. They took the lead after a little while when Beckham scored from quite far out. He scored again and again after the midway point. Official attendance was "as many as the stadium holds."

Football results

Spain: a lot of goals
Italy: not quite so many

Colombia: no goals
Nigeria: some goals

Germany: a few goals
Thailand: the same few goals

Mexico: tons and tons of goals
Sweden: even more goals

EXTRA!
India babies
—and another!

Olympic Athletes Win Gold

Sonia Marx

Ima Springyleg won a gold medal at the Olympic games yesterday with a record-breaking high jump. She beat the previous record of very high indeed by jumping a bit higher still.

Also at the Olympics, Harry Foot won gold and broke the world record for the short sprint, when he beat several other runners in a race across a medium-sized field. Silver went to Jimmy Cricket, who finished just a whisker behind Foot. A veteran athlete, Cricket has now won at least several Olympic medals.

How did counting begin?

When people first started counting, they almost certainly used their hands. Since most people have **ten fingers** to count with, it made sense to count in tens, and this is how our modern counting system (the decimal system) began.

Why use hands?

Fingers gave people a handy way of **counting** even before they had words for numbers. Touching fingers while you count helps you keep track, and by holding fingers in the air you can **communicate** numbers without needing words. The link between fingers and numbers is very ancient. Even today, we use the Latin word for finger (digit) to mean number.

What's base 10?

Mathematicians say we count in **base ten**, which means we count in groups of ten. There's no mathematical reason why we have to count in tens, it's just an accident of biology. If **aliens** with only eight fingers exist, they probably count in base eight.

Did cavemen count?

For most of history, people actually had little need for numbers. Before **farming** was invented, people lived as "hunter-gatherers," collecting food from the wild. They gathered only what they needed and had little left over to trade or hoard, so there wasn't much point in counting things. However, they may have had a sense of time from watching the sun, moon, and stars.

Members of the the **Pirahã tribe** in the Amazon rainforest don't count past **two**

If people only had 8 *fingers* and *thumbs*, we'd probably count in base eight

Some **ancient cultures** used their hands to count in **base five**

Can everyone count?

In a few places, people still live as hunter-gatherers. Most modern hunter-gatherers can count, but some **hardly bother**. The Pirahã tribe in the Amazon rain forest only **counts to two**—all bigger numbers are "many." In Tanzania, the Hadza tribe **counts to three**. Both tribes manage fine without big numbers, which they never seem to need.

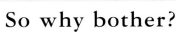

So why bother?

If people can live without numbers, why did we start counting? The main reason was to catch **cheaters**. Imagine catching 10 fish and asking a friend to carry them home. If you couldn't count, your friend could **steal** some and you'd never know.

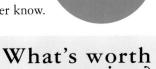

What's worth counting?

Even when people had invented counting and gotten used to the idea, they probably only counted things that seemed valuable. Some tribal people still do this. The Yupno people in Papua New Guinea count string bags, grass skirts, pigs, and money, but not days, people, sweet potatoes, or nuts!

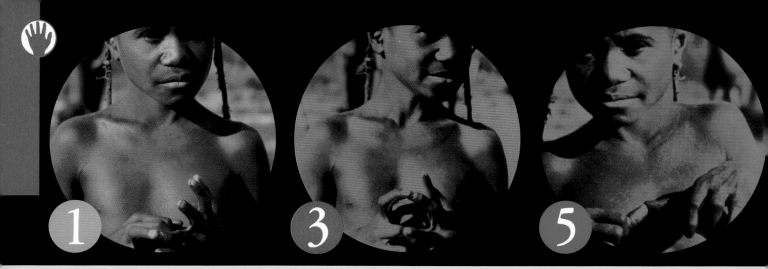

You can *count* on PEOPLE

HANDS AND FEET

The tribes of Papua New Guinea have at least **900 different counting systems**. Many tribes count past their fingers and so don't use base ten. One tribe counts toes after fingers, giving them a base 20 system. Their word for 10 is *two hands*. Fifteen is *two hands and one foot*, and 20 is *one man*.

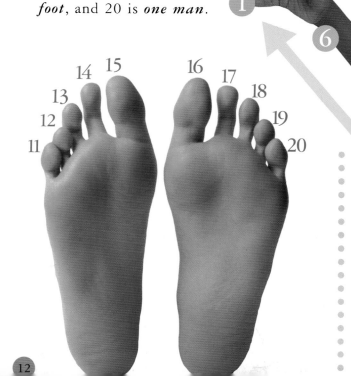

Head and shoulders

In some parts of Papua New Guinea, tribal people start counting on a little finger and then cross the hand, arm, and body before running down the other arm. The Faiwol tribe counts 27 body parts and uses the words for body parts as numbers. The word for 14 is *nose*, for instance. For numbers bigger than 27, they add *one man*. So 40 would be *one man and right eye*.

START HERE!

Counting on your hands is fine for numbers up to ten, but what about bigger numbers? Throughout history, people invented lots of different ways of counting past ten, often by using different parts of the body. In some parts of the world, people still count on their bodies today.

IN THE SIXTIES

The Babylonians, who lived in Iraq about 5,000 years ago, counted in base 60. They gave their year 360 days, which is 6 × 60. We don't know for sure how they used their hands to count, but one theory is that they used a thumb to tap the 12 finger segments of that hand, and fingers on the other hand to count lots of 12, making 60 altogether. Babylonians invented *minutes* and *seconds*, which we still count in sixties today.

MAKING A POINT

Counting on the body is so important to some tribal people that they can't count properly in words alone. The **Baruga** tribe in Papua New Guinea counts with 22 body parts but uses the same word, *finger*, for the numbers 2, 3, 4, 19, 20, and 21. So to avoid confusion, they have to point at the correct finger whenever they say these numbers.

A HANDY TRICK

Hands are handy for multiplying as well as counting. Use this trick to remember your nine-times table. First, hold your hands in front of your face and number the fingers 1 to 10, counting from the left. To work out any number times nine, simply fold down that finger. For instance, to work out 7 × 9, fold the seventh finger. Now there are 6 fingers on the left and 3 on the right, so the answer is 63.

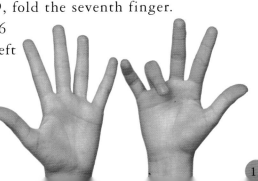

Making a *mark*

For hundreds of thousands of years, people managed fine by counting with their hands. But about 6,000 years ago, the world changed. In the **Middle East**, people figured out how to tame animals and plant crops—they became farmers.

BABYLONIAN *numbers*

About 6,000 years ago, the farmers in Babylonia (Iraq) started making clay tokens as records of deals. They had different-shaped tokens for different things ...

... so an **oval** might stand for a **sack of wheat** ...

... and a circle might mean a **jar of oil**. For two or three jars of oil, two or three tokens were exchanged.

When a deal involved several tokens, they were wrapped together in a clay envelope. To show what was inside, the trader made symbols on the outside with a pointed stick. Then someone had the bright idea of simply marking clay with symbols and not bothering with tokens at all. And that's how writing was invented.

Quipu, South America

Once farming started, people began trading in markets. They had to remember exactly how many things they owned, sold, and bought, otherwise people would cheat each other. So the farmers started **keeping records**. To do this, they could make **notches in sticks or bones ...**

Ishango Bone from Africa

... or knots in string.

In Iraq, they made marks in lumps of wet clay from a river. When the clay hardened in the sun, it made a permanent record.

In doing this, the farmers of Iraq invented not just written numbers but writing itself. It was the start of civilization—and it was all triggered by numbers.

4000–2000 BC

The first symbols were circles and cones like the old tokens, but as the Babylonians got better at sharpening their wooden pens, the symbols turned into small, sharp wedges.

For a ONE they made a mark like this:

To write numbers up to nine, they simply made more marks:

2 was   3 was   4 was

When they got to **10**, they turned the symbol on its side ...

... and when they got to **60**, they turned it upright again.

So this is how the Babylonians would have written the number **99**:

60   30   9   = 99

Work like an *Egyptian*

HAIRSBREADTH
(the smallest unit)

INCH

7 PALMS

CUBIT

PALM

YARD   FOOT

The ancient Egyptians farmed the thin ribbon of green land by the **Nile River,** which crosses the **Sahara Desert.** The Nile used to flood every summer, washing away fields and ditches. Year after year, the Egyptians had to mark out their fields anew. And so they became expert surveyors and timekeepers, using math not just for counting but for measuring land, making buildings, and tracking time.

To measure anything—whether it's time, weight, or distance—you need units. The Egyptians based their units for length on the human body. Even today, many people still measure their height in "feet."

Egyptian numbers weren't suited to doing fractions, so the Egyptians divided each unit into smaller units. One cubit was made of 7 palms, for instance, and a palm was made of 4 digits.

EGYPTIAN *numbers*

Egyptians counted in base 10 and wrote numbers as little pictures, or "hieroglyphs." Simple lines stood for 1, 10, and 100. For 1,000 they drew a lotus flower; 10,000 was a finger; 100,000 was a frog; and a million was a god.

1
10
100
1000
10,000
100,000
1,000,000

The hieroglyphics were stacked up in piles to create bigger numbers. This is how the Egyptians wrote 1,996:

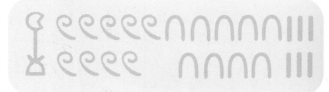

While hieroglyphics were carved in stone, a different system was used for writing on paper.

Without math, *the pyramids* would never have been built

A circle formed with the pyramid's

Perimeter ÷ height = 2 × pi

height × height = area of side

Sloping side ÷ by half the base = phi

height as radius has the same perimeter as the base

It was their skill at math that enabled the Egyptians to build the pyramids. The Great Pyramid of Khufu is a mathematical wonder. Built into its dimensions are the sacred numbers pi and phi, which mystified the mathematicians of ancient Greece (see pages 36 and 44 for more about pi and phi). Maybe this is just a coincidence, but if it isn't, the Egyptians were very good at math. Two million blocks of stone were cut by hand to make this amazing building—enough to make a 7- foot (2-meter) wall from Egypt to the North Pole. It was the largest and tallest building in the world for 3,500 years, until the Eiffel Tower topped it in 1895.

TAMING TIME

Knowing when the Nile was going to flood was vital to the Egyptian farmers. As a result, they learned to count the days and keep careful track of the date. They used the moon and stars as a calendar. When the star Sirius rose in summer, they knew the Nile was about to flood. The next new moon was the beginning of the Egyptian year.

Egyptians also used the sun and stars as clocks. They divided night and day into 12 hours each, though the length of the hours varied with the seasons. Thanks to the Egyptians, we have 24 hours in a day.

3000–1000 BC

Egyptian numbers were fine for adding and subtracting, but they were hopeless for multiplying.

To get around this, the Egyptians devised an ingenious way of multiplying by doubling. Once you know this trick, you can use it yourself.

Say you want to know 13×23. You need to write two columns of numbers. In the left column, write $1, 2, 4$, and so on, doubling as much as you can without going past 13. In the right column, start with the second number. Double it until the columns are the same size. On the left, you can make 13 only one way $(8+4+1)$, so cross out the other numbers. Cross out the corresponding numbers on the right, then add up what's left.

13	×	23
1		23
2̶		4̶6̶
4		92
8		184 +
13		299

MAYAN *numbers*

Native Americans also discovered farming and invented ways of writing numbers. The Mayans had a number system even better than that of the Egyptians. They kept perfect track of the date and calculated that a year is 365.242 days long. They counted in **twenties**, perhaps using toes as well as fingers. Their numbers look like beans, sticks, and shells—objects they may once have used like an abacus.

1
2
3
4
5

The symbols for 1–4 looked like cocoa beans or pebbles. The symbol for 5 looked like a stick.

The sticks and beans were piled up in groups to make numbers up to 20, so 18 would be:

ROMAN *numbers*

Roman numbers spread across Europe during the Roman empire. The Romans counted in tens and used letters as numerals. For Europeans, this was the main way of writing numbers for 2,000 years. We still see Roman numbers today in clocks, the names of royalty (like Queen Elizabeth II), and books with paragraphs numbered (i), (ii), and (iii).

Like most counting systems, Roman numbers start off as a tally:

1 is **I**   2 is **II**   3 is **III**

Different letters are then used for bigger numerals:

V	X	L	C	D	M
5	10	50	100	500	1000

250–900 AD

For numbers bigger than
20, Mayans arranged their sticks and beans in layers. Our numbers are written horizontally, but the Mayans worked **vertically**. The bottom layer showed units up to 20. The next layer showed twenties, and the layer above that showed 400s. So 421 would be:

400
20
1

A shell was used for zero,
so 418 would be

400

400
NO twenties

18

Mayan numbers
were good for doing addition. You simply added up the sticks and stones in each layer to work out the final number. So, 418 + 2,040 was done like this:

400s

20s

1s

 **+** **=**

418   +   2,040   =   2,458

500 BC to 1500 AD

To write any number, you make
a list of letters that add up to the right amount, with small numerals on the right and large on the left. It's simple, but the numbers can get long and cumbersome.

To write 49 you need 9 letters:

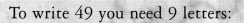

XXXXVIIII

To make things a bit easier, the Romans invented a rule that
allowed you to **subtract** a small numeral when it's on the left of a larger one. So instead of writing **IIII** for 4, you write **IV**. People didn't always stick to the rule though, and even today you'll see the number 4 written as **IIII** on clocks (though clocks also show 9 as **IX**).

For sums like division and multiplication, Roman numerals were **appalling**. This is how you work out 123 × 165:

			CXXIII
			CLXV
	D	LL	VVV
	M	CC	XXX
	MMMM	DD	LLL
MMMMMMMMMMM	CCC	
MMMMMMMMMMMMMMMMMM	DDD CCCCC LLLLL XXX VVV
	CCCCCC	L	XXXX V
DDDD			*the answer*
MMMMMMMMMMMMMMMMMMM			*is 20,295*
MMMMMMMMMMMMMMMMMMMMCCLXXXXV			

In fact, Roman numbers probably held back math for years. It wasn't until the amazingly clever **Indian** way of counting came to Europe that math really took off.

INDIAN *numbers*

In ancient times, the best way of adding was with an abacus—a calculating device made of rows of beads or stones. But about 1,500 years ago, people in India had a better idea. They invented a "place system"—a way of writing numbers so that the symbols matched the rows on an abacus. This meant you could do tricky sums **without** an abacus, just by writing numbers down. A symbol was needed for an empty row, so the Indians invented **zero**. It was a stroke of genius. The new numbers spread from Asia to Europe and became *the numbers we use today*.

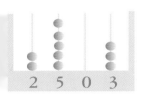

2 5 0 3

Unlike other number systems, the Indian system had only **10 symbols**, which made it wonderfully simple. These symbols changed over the centuries as they spread from place to place, gradually evolving into the modern digits we all now use.

300 BC to 400 AD	400 AD to 600 AD	700 AD to 1100	900 AD to 1200	16th century
—	—	٩	۱	1
=	=	٢	۲	۲
≡	≡	३	३	३
Ƴ	೪	४	¿	੪
┠	┡	५	९	5
५	൜	६	६	σ
7	ๆ	۽	౧	7
५	ၒ	८	४	੪
౨	3	੬	९	9
		0	0	0

EUROPE 1200 to NOW Indian numbers slowly replaced Roman numbers in Europe as people discovered how useful they were for calculating. The new numbers helped trigger the Renaissance, or "age of learning"—the period of history in which modern science was born.

ENGLAND 1100 AD Adelard of Bath, an English monk, visited North Africa disguised as an Arab. He translated Al Khwarizmi's books and brought zero back to England. He only told other monks, so nothing happened.

NORTH AFRICA 1200 AD Indian numbers were picked up by Italian merchants visiting the Arab countries of North Africa. In 1202 an Italian named Fibonacci explained how the numbers worked in a book called *Liber Abaci*, and so helped the Indian system spread to Italy.

200 BC to now

The Indians wrote their numbers on palm leaves with ink, using a flowing style that made the numbers curly. The symbols for 2 and 3 were groups of lines at first, but the lines joined up when people wrote them quickly:

From this...   *to this...*   *...to this.*

NOTHING *comes to Europe*

BAGHDAD 800 AD

Indian numbers and zero spread to Baghdad, which was the center of the newly founded Muslim empire. A man called Al Khwarizmi wrote books about math and helped spread Indian numbers and zero to the rest of the world. The words "arithmetic" and "algorithm" come from his name, and the word "algebra" comes from his book *Ilm al-jabr wa'l muqabalah*.

We sometimes call modern numbers *Arabic*, because they spread to Europe through the Arab world

INDIA
200 BC to 600 AD
Mathematicians in India were using separate symbols for 1 to 9 as early as 300 BC. By 600 AD they had invented a place system and zero.

BAGHDAD

INDIA

The Muslim empire spread across Africa, taking zero with it.

Merchants traveling by camel train or boat took the Indian number system west.

Nothing really MATTERS

Zero doesn't always mean *nothing*. If you put a zero on the end of a number, that multiplies it by ten. That's because we use a "place system" in which the *position* of a digit tells you its value. The number 123, for instance, means one lot of a hundred, two lots of ten, and 3 ones. We need zero whenever there are gaps to fill. Otherwise, we wouldn't be able to tell 11 from 101.

A misbehaving *number*

Ask someone this question: "What's $1 \times 2 \times 3 \times 4 \times 5 \times 6 \times 7 \times 8 \times 9 \times 0$?" The answer, of course, is zero, but if you don't listen carefully it sounds like an impossibly hard problem. Multiplying by zero is easy, but dividing by zero leads to trouble. If you try it on the calculator built into a computer, the calculator may well tell you off or give you a strange answer like "infinity"!

Dividing equations by zero leads to impossible conclusions. For instance, take this equation:

$$1 \times 0 = 0$$

If you divide both sides by zero, you get

$$1 = 0 \div 0$$

But if you start with this equation...

$$2 \times 0 = 0$$

... and do the same thing, you get

$$2 = 0 \div 0$$

So 1 and 2 equal the same amount, which means that

$$1 = 2$$

And that's impossible. So what went wrong? The answer is that you CAN'T divide by zero, because it doesn't make sense. Think about it—it makes sense to ask, "How many times does 2 go into 6?", but not to ask "How many times does nothing go into 6?".

Happy New Year!

Zero was invented about 1,500 years ago, but it's still causing **headaches** even though we've been using it for centuries. When everyone celebrated **New Year's Eve** in 1999, they thought they were celebrating the beginning of a new millennium.

But since there wasn't a year zero, the celebration was a year early. The new millennium and the 21st century actually began on January 1, 2001, not January 1, 2000.

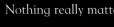

2000 BC

4,000 years ago in Iraq, the **Babylonians** showed zeros by leaving small gaps between wedge marks on clay, but they didn't think of the gaps as numbers in their own right.

Babylonia

India

350 BC The ancient Greeks were brilliant at math, but they **hated** the idea of zero. The Greek philosopher Aristotle said zero should be **illegal** because it made a mess of equations when he tried to divide by it.

1 AD The Romans didn't have a zero because their counting system didn't need one. After all, if there's nothing to count, why would you need a number? (Some people used to think the number 1 was also pointless, since you only have a...

...number of things if you have more than one.) Even if the Romans had thought of zero, it wouldn't have worked with their cumbersome counting system, which used long lists of letters like **MMCCCXVCXIII.**

a BRIEF **HISTORY** of **NOTHING**

Central America

North Africa

600 AD Indian mathematicians invented the modern zero. They had a counting system in which the **position** of a digit affected its value, and they used dots or circles to show gaps. **Why a circle?** Because Indians once used pebbles in sand to add and subtract, and a circle looked like the gap where a pebble had been removed.

Arabia

Europe

1150 AD Zero came to Europe in the 12th century, when Indian numerals spread from Arab countries. People soon realized that doing math was much easier when you have *nothing* to help you count!

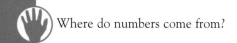

A world of numbers

	1	2	3	4	5	6	7	8	9
Babylonian	∀	∀∀	∀∀∀	∀∀∀∀	∀∀∀∀∀	∀∀∀∀∀∀	∀∀∀∀∀∀∀	∀∀∀∀∀∀∀∀	∀∀∀∀∀∀∀∀∀
Egyptian hieroglyphic	I	II	III	IIII	IIIII	IIIIII	IIIIIII	IIIIIIII	IIIIIIIII
Egyptian script	I	U	III	IIII	Ϣ	ϢϢ	𝘻	=	Ϣ𝘻
Chinese rod	I	II	III	IIII	IIIII	丅	丌	丌丨	丌丌
Chinese script	一	二	三	四	五	六	七	八	九
Hindu (Gwalior)	?	?	?	8	५	६	?	?	९
Hebrew	א	ב	ג	ד	ה	ו	ז	ח	ט
Greek	A	B	Γ	Δ	E	F	Z	H	Θ
Roman	I	II	III	IV	V	VI	VII	VIII	IX
Mayan	•	••	•••	••••	—	·	··	···	····
Modern Arabic	١	٢	٣	٤	٥	٦	٧	٨	٩

People have invented hundreds of "number alphabets" throughout history, and a few of the important ones are shown here. They're very different, but they do have some interesting things in common. Most began with a tally of simple marks, like lines or dots. And most had a change of style at 10—the number for two full hands.

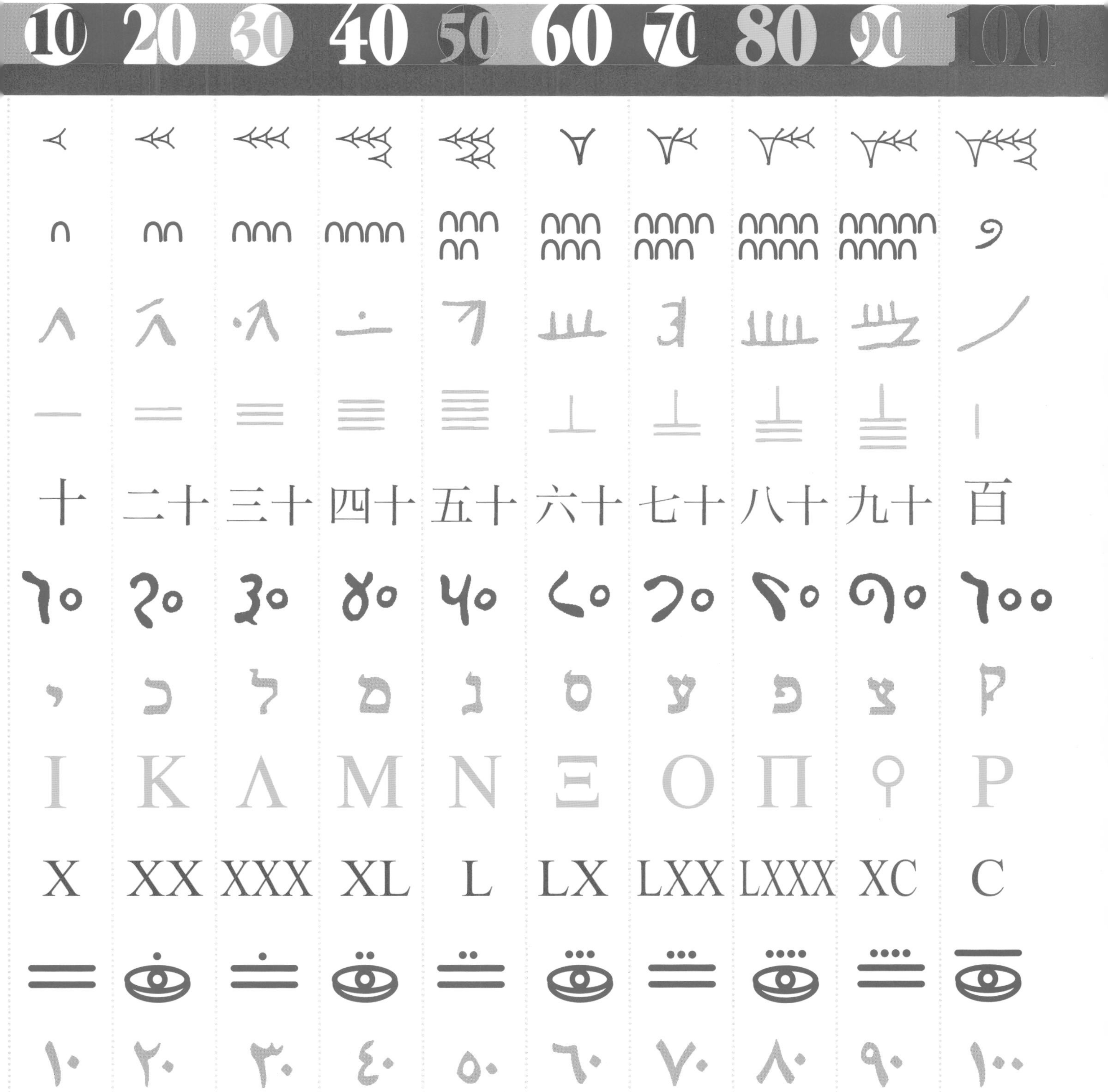

10	20	30	40	50	60	70	80	90	100

BIG
number quiz

Try this math quiz, but **watch out** for **trick** questions! The **answers** are in the **back** of the book.

1 If there are three pizzas and you take away two, how many do you have?

2 One costs $1, 12 is $2, and it costs you $3 to get 400. What are they?

The top questions are fairly easy

the bottom questions are a little more ...

12 Mrs. Peabody the farmer's wife takes a basket of eggs to the farmer's market. Mrs. Black buys half the eggs plus half an egg. Mr. Smith buys half the remaining eggs plus half an egg. Then Mrs. Lee buys half the remaining eggs plus half an egg. Mr. Jackson does the same, and then so does Mrs. Fishface. There's now one egg left and none of the eggs was broken or halved. How many were there to begin with?
Clue: work out the answer backward

13 Three friends share a meal at a restaurant and pay the check of $30. But the waiter realizes he's made a mistake and should have charged $25. He takes $5 from the cash register to give it back, but on his way he decides to keep $2 as a tip and give each customer $1, since you can't divide $5 by 3. So, each customer ends up paying $9 and the waiter keeps $2, making $29 in total. What happened to the missing $1?

14 Four boys have to cross a rickety rope bridge over a canyon at night to reach a train station. They have to hurry because their train leaves in 17 minutes. Anyone crossing the bridge must carry a flashlight to look for missing planks, but the boys only have one flashlight and can't throw it back across because the canyon is too wide. There's just enough room for them to walk in pairs. Each boy walks at a different speed, and a pair must walk at the speed of the slowest one.
William can cross in 1 minute
Arthur can cross in 2 minutes
Charlie can cross in 5 minutes
Benedict can cross in 10 minutes
How do they do it?
Clue: put the slowest two together

15 In under two minutes, can you think of any 4 odd numbers (including repeated numbers) that add up to 19?

16 A cowboy has 11 horses that he wants to divide between his sons. He's promised his oldest son half the horses, his middle son a quarter of the horses, and his youngest son a sixth of the horses. How can he divide the

3 You're driving a train from Boston to Washington, DC. You leave at 9:00 a.m. and travel for 2½ hours. There's a half-hour stop in New York, then the train continues for another 2 hours. What's the driver's name?

4 What's 50 divided by a half?

5 If you have three apples and you eat one every half-hour, how long will they last?

6 There are 30 crows in a field. The farmer shoots 4. How many are in the field now?

7 A giant tub of ice cream weighs 6 lb plus half its weight. How much does it weigh in total?

8 A man lives next to a circular park. It takes him 80 minutes to walk around it in a clockwise direction but 1 hour 20 minutes to walk the other direction. Why?

9 How many animals of each sex did Moses take on the Ark?

10 A man has 14 camels and all but three die. How many are left?

11 How many birthdays does the average man have?

challenging

horses fairly, without killing any?
Clue: the cowboy's neighbor has a horse for sale, but the cowboy doesn't have any money to buy it.

17 I have a 5-gallon pail and a 3-gallon pail. How can I measure out exactly 4 gallons of water from a faucet if I have no other containers?

18 Find two numbers that multiply together to give 1,000,000 but neither of which contains any zeros.
Clue: halving will help

19 A gold chain breaks into 4 sections, each with 3 links. It looks like this: ⬤⬤⬤ ⬤⬤⬤ ⬤⬤⬤ ⬤⬤⬤. You take the chain to a shop to have it mended. Opening a link costs $1 and closing a link costs $1. You have $6. Is that enough to turn the broken chain back into a complete circle?

20 A teacher explains to her class how roman numerals work. Then she writes "IX" on the blackboard and asks how to make it into 6 by adding a single line, without lifting the chalk

once. How can you do it?
Clue: be creative

21 What row of numbers comes next?
1
11
21
1211
111221
312211
13112221
Clue: read the digits out loud. As you read each line, look at the line above.

22 A zookeeper was asked how many camels and ostriches were in his zoo. This was his answer: "Among the camels and ostriches there are 60 eyes and 86 feet." How many of each kind of animal were there?
Clue: think about the eyes first

MAGIC numbers

"The world's first magicians were people who could work magic with math. They could tell the date and predict the seasons not by magic, but by counting the days and watching the moon and stars.

People are still fascinated by magic today. We like to imagine what it would be like to cast spells and use magical powers. Well, math can help you do truly magical things. Being a mathematician makes you a mathemagician, because math is magical.

In this section you can find out about magic numbers like pi, infinity, and prime numbers. And you can learn how to perform mathemagical tricks that will baffle and amaze your friends."

MAGIC SQUARES

In a magic square, the numbers in every row and column add up to the same amount—the "magic sum". Look at the square on the right and see if you can work out the magic sum. Does it work for every row and column? Now try adding...

- the two diagonals
- the 4 numbers in any corner
- the 4 corner numbers
- the 4 center numbers

In fact, there are 86 ways of picking 4 numbers that add to 34. This was the first magic square to be published in Europe, and it appeared in a painting in 1514. The artist even managed to include the year!

16	3	2	13
5	10	11	8
9	6	7	12
4	15	14	1

The world's oldest magic square was invented by the Chinese emperor Yu the Great 4,000 years ago, using the numbers 1 to 9. To create this square yourself, write 1–9 in order, swap opposite corners, and squeeze the square into a diamond shape.

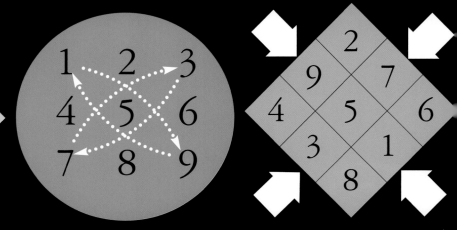

Birthday square

You can adapt the magic square below so that the numbers add to any number bigger than 22. The secret is to change just the four highlighted numbers. At the moment, the magic sum is 22. Suppose you want to change it to 30. Because 30 is 8 more than 22, just add 8 to the highlighted numbers and draw out the square again. It always works!

8	11	2	1
1	2	7	12
3	4	9	6
10	5	4	3

Use this magic square to make a birthday card, with the numbers adding up to the person's age.

Upside-down square

96	11	89	68
88	69	91	16
61	86	18	99
19	98	66	81

See if you can work out the magic sum for this very unusual square. Then turn the page upside down and look at the square again. Does it still work?

A KNIGHT'S TOUR

In the magic square below, the rows and columns add up to 260. But there's something even more surprising about this square. Look at the pattern the numbers make as you count from 1 upward. Each move is like the move of a knight on a chessboard: two steps forward and one step to the side.

1	48	31	50	33	16	63	18
30	51	46	3	62	19	14	35
47	2	49	32	15	34	17	64
52	29	4	45	20	61	36	13
5	44	25	56	9	40	21	60
28	53	8	41	24	57	12	37
43	6	55	26	39	10	59	22
54	27	42	7	58	23	38	11

Make your own

magic square by using knight's moves. Draw a 5×5 grid and put a 1 anywhere in the bottom row. Fill in higher numbers by making knight's moves up and right. If you leave the grid, reenter on the opposite side. If you can't make a knight's move, jump two squares to the right instead.

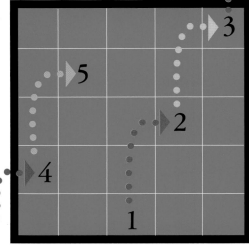

If you're stuck on the puzzle above, here's a clue: try adding. This famous series of numbers was found by Leonardo Fibonacci of Pisa, in Italy, 800 years ago. It crops up in the most surprising places.

Nature's NUMBERS

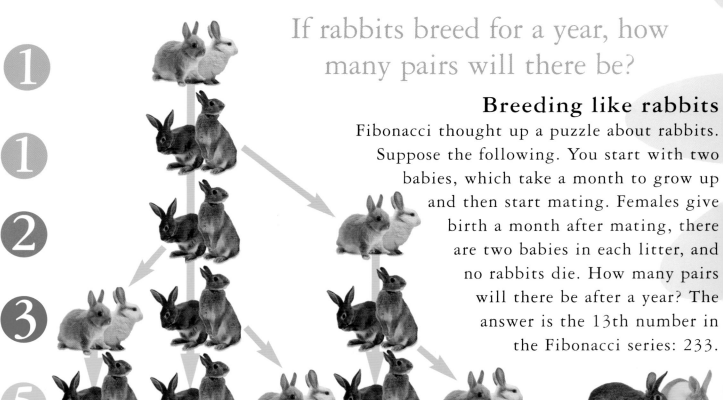

If rabbits breed for a year, how many pairs will there be?

1

1

2

3

5

Breeding like rabbits

Fibonacci thought up a puzzle about rabbits. Suppose the following. You start with two babies, which take a month to grow up and then start mating. Females give birth a month after mating, there are two babies in each litter, and no rabbits die. How many pairs will there be after a year? The answer is the 13th number in the Fibonacci series: 233.

Count the petals

The number of petals in a flower is often a number from the Fibonacci sequence. Michaelmas daisies, for instance, usually have either 34, 55, or 89 petals.

Counting spirals

Fibonacci numbers are common in flower-heads. If you look closely at the coneflower below, you'll see that the small florets are arranged in spirals running **clockwise** and **counterclockwise**. The number of spirals in each direction is a Fibonacci number. In this case, there are 21 clockwise spirals and 34 counterclockwise spirals.

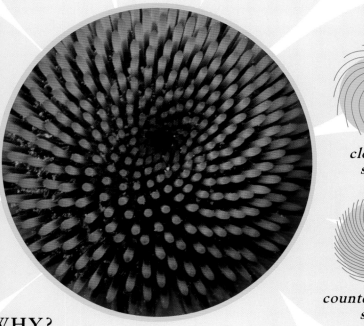

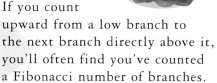

clockwise spirals

counterclockwise spirals

WHY?

Why do Fibonacci numbers keep cropping up in nature? In the case of rabbits, they don't. Rabbits actually have more than two babies per litter and breed much more quickly than in Fibonacci's famous puzzle. But the numbers do crop up a lot in plants. They happen because they provide the best way for packing seeds, petals, or leaves into a limited space without large gaps or awkward overlaps.

Cauliflowers and cones

It's not just flowers that contain **Fibonacci spirals**. You can see the same patterns in **pine cones**, **pineapple skin**, **broccoli florets**, and **cauliflowers**. Fibonacci numbers also appear in leaves, branches, and stalks. Plants often produce branches in a winding pattern as they grow. If you count upward from a low branch to the next branch directly above it, you'll often find you've counted a Fibonacci number of branches.

Musical numbers

One octave on a piano keyboard is made up of 13 keys: **8 white keys** and **5 black keys**, which are split into groups of 3 and 2. Funnily enough, all of these are Fibonacci numbers. It's another amazing Fibonacci coincidence!

The Fibonacci sequence is closely related to the number 1.618034, which is known as **phi** (say "fie"). Mathematicians and artists have known about this very peculiar number for several thousand years, and for a long time people thought it had magical properties.

Leonardo da Vinci called phi the "golden ratio" and used it in paintings

the Golden RATIO

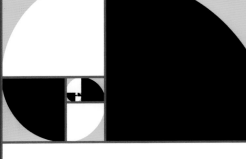

GOLDEN SPIRALS

If you draw a rectangle with sides 1 and phi units long, you'll have what artists call a "golden rectangle"— supposedly the most beautiful rectangle possible. Divide this into a square and a rectangle (like the red lines here), and the small rectangle is yet another golden rectangle. If you keep doing this, a spiral pattern begins to emerge. This "golden spiral" looks similar to the shell of a sea creature called a nautilus, but in fact they aren't quite the same. A nautilus shell gets about phi times wider with each half-turn, while a golden spiral gets phi times wider with each quarter-turn.

Golden rectangles create a spiral that continues forever

Golden rectangle

WHAT IS PHI?

Draw a straight line 10 centimeters long, then make a small mark on it 6.18 centimeters along. You've divided the line into two sections. If you divide the length of the whole line by the length of the long section, you'll get the number 1.618. And if you divide the length of the long section by the length of the short section, you'll get the same ratio. This is the *golden ratio*, or phi, written **Φ**.

◄ • • • • • • • • • • • *6.18 cm* • • • • • • • • • • • ►

◄ • • • • • • • • • • • • • • • • • • *10 cm* • • • • • • • • • • • • • • • • ►

Phantastic phi

Phi has strange properties. Multiplying it by itself, for instance, is exactly the same as adding one. If you divide any number in the Fibonacci series by the one before, you'll get a ratio close to phi. This ratio gets closer to phi as you travel along the series, but it never quite gets there. In fact, it's impossible to write phi as a ratio of two numbers, so mathematicians call it "irrational." If you tried to write phi as a decimal, its decimal places would go on forever.

$$1 \div \Phi = \Phi - 1$$
$$\Phi \times \Phi = \Phi + 1$$

FAQ

What's magic about phi?

Ancient Greeks thought phi was magic because it kept cropping up in shapes they considered sacred. In a five-pointed star, for instance, the ratio between long and short lines is phi exactly.

Why did artists use phi?

Leonardo da Vinci and other artists of medieval Europe were fascinated by math. They thought shapes involving phi had the most visually pleasing proportions, so they often worked them into paintings.

Building with phi

Ancient Greek architects are said to have used phi in buildings. Some people claim the Parthenon (below) in Athens is based on golden rectangles. What do you think?

BIG NUMBERS

A thousand has three zeros, a million has six. Each time you add three more zeros, you reach a number with a new name. →

thousand
million
billion
trillion
quadrillion
quintillion
sexillion

How many drops of water make an ocean? How many atoms are there in your body? How many grains of sand would fill the universe? Some numbers are so big we can't imagine them or even write them down. Mathematicians cope with these whoppers by using "*powers*."

WHAT ARE POWERS?

A power is a tiny number written just next to another number, like this: ⤷

It means "4 to the power of 2."

4^2

The power tells you how many times to multiply the main number by itself. 4^2 means multiply two fours together: 4×4, which is 16. And 4^3 means $4 \times 4 \times 4$, which is 64.

Power crazy

Powers are handy because they make it easy to write down numbers that would otherwise be much too long. Take the number 9^{9^9}, for instance, which means 9 to the power of 9 to the power of 9, or $9^{387,420,489}$. If you wrote this in full, you'd need 369 million digits and a piece of paper 500 miles (800 km) long.

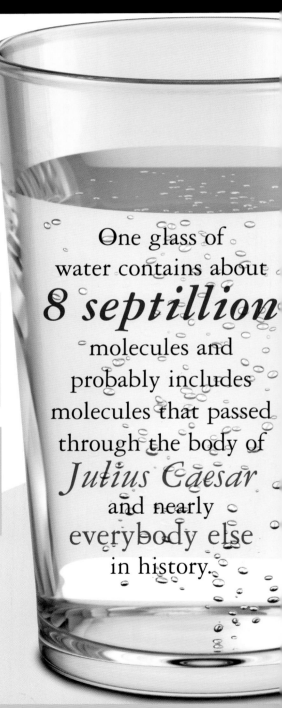

One glass of water contains about **8 *septillion*** molecules and probably includes molecules that passed through the body of *Julius Caesar* and nearly everybody else in history.

1 GOOGOL = 10,000,000,000,000,000,000,000,000,000,000,000,000,000,00

septillion
octillion
nonillion
decillion
undecillion
duodecillion
tredecillion

quattuordecillion
quindecillion
sexdecillion
septdecillion,
octodecillion
novemdecillion
vigintillion

unvigintillion
duovigintillion
trevigintillion
quattuorvigintillion
quinvigintillion
sexvigintillion
septvigintillion

octovigintillion
novemvigintillion
trigintillion
untrigintillion
duotrigintillion

googol

Get rich quick

Imagine you put *1 penny* on the first square of chessboard, 2¢ on the next square, then 4, 8 and so on, doubling each time. By the last square, how much would you have? You can work it out with powers. The chessboard has 64 squares, so you double your penny 63 times. The final amount, therefore, is 2^{63} cents, or **90,000 trillion dollars**. And that's more than all the money in the world!

Counting sand

The Greek mathematician Archimedes tried to work out how many grains of sand would fill the universe. The answer was a lot. In fact, to work it out, Archimedes had to invent a new way of counting that used colossal numbers called **myriads** (1 myriad = 10,000), which worked like powers.

By Archimedes' reckoning, you'd need 10^{63} (1 *vigintillion*) sand grains to fill the universe

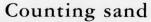

FIND OUT MORE

Standard form

To keep things simple, scientists usually write big numbers in **powers of ten**—a system called standard form. So instead of writing 9,000,000,000 (9 billion), a scientist would write 9×10^9. Most calculators show numbers in standard form when they get too big to fit on the screen.

Googols & beyond

Googol! The Internet search engine Google is named after a *googol*—a number made of a 1 followed by a hundred zeros. A mathematician named **Edward Kasner** gave this number its name. He asked his 9-year-old nephew for a suggestion, and the answer was "googol." Kasner's nephew also thought up **googolplex**, now the official name for 1 followed by a googol zeros. This number is so ridiculously huge it has no practical use. There isn't enough room in the universe to write it down, even if each digit was smaller than an atom.

0,000,000,000,000,000,000,000,000,000,000,000,000,000,000,000,000

infinity and *beyond*

What's the biggest number you can think of? Whatever answer you come up with, you can always add 1. Then you can add 1 again, and again, and again... In fact, there's no limit to how big (or how small) numbers can get. The word mathematicians use for this endlessness is **infinity**.

An *infinite* amount of time is called an *eternity*

the symbol for infinity looks like a figure 8 on its side

How long is an infinite distance? Imagine you can run a *million miles an hour* and you spend a *billion lifetimes* running nonstop in a straight line. By the end of your run, you'd be **no closer** to infinity than when you started.

Concepts like infinity and eternity are very difficult for the human mind to comprehend—they're just *too big*. To picture how long an eternity lasts, imagine a single ant

THE MIRACULOUS JAR

Infinity is weird. Imagine a jar containing an infinite amount of candy.

If you take a piece out, *how many* are left?

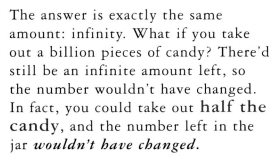

The answer is exactly the same amount: infinity. What if you take out a billion pieces of candy? There'd still be an infinite amount left, so the number wouldn't have changed. In fact, you could take out **half the candy**, and the number left in the jar *wouldn't have changed*.

Mathematicians use the symbol ∞ to mean INFINITY, so we can sum up the strange jar of sweets like this:

$$\infty - 1 = \infty$$
$$\infty + 1 = \infty$$
$$\infty - 1,000,000,000 = \infty$$
$$\infty \div 2 = \infty$$
$$\infty \times \infty = \infty$$

But infinity isn't exactly a number—it's really just an idea. And that's why sums involving infinity don't always make sense.

FIND OUT MORE

Hilbert's Hotel

Mathematician **David Hilbert** thought up an imaginary hotel to show the math of infinity. Suppose the hotel has an infinite number of rooms but all are full. A guest arrives and asks for a room. The owner thinks for a minute, then asks all the residents to move one room up. The person in room 1 moves to room 2, the person in room 2 moves to room 3, and so on. This leaves a spare room for the new guest.

The next day, an infinitely long bus arrives with an infinite number of new guests. The owner has to think hard, but he cracks the problem again. He asks all guests to double their room number and move to the new number. The residents all end up in rooms with even numbers, leaving an infinite number of odd-numbered rooms free.

Beyond infinity

Strange as it may sound, there are different kinds of infinity, and some are bigger than others. Things you can count, like whole numbers (1, 2, 3...), make a **countable** infinity. But in between these are endless peculiar numbers like phi and pi, whose decimals places never end. These "irrational numbers" make an **uncountable** infinity, which, according to the experts, is infinitely bigger than ordinary infinity. So infinity is bigger than infinity!

walking around Planet Earth over and over again. Suppose it takes one footstep every million years. By the time the ant's feet have worn down the Earth to the size of pea, eternity has not even *begun*.

PRIME suspects

A *prime* **number** is a whole number that you can't divide into other whole numbers except for 1.

The number 23 is prime, for instance, because nothing will divide into it without leaving a remainder. But 22 isn't: 11 and 2 will divide into it. Some mathematicians call prime numbers the building blocks of math because you can create ***all other*** whole numbers by multiplying primes together. Here are some examples:

$$55 = 5 \times 11$$
$$75 = 3 \times 5 \times 5$$
$$39 = 3 \times 13$$
$$221 = 13 \times 17$$

31 is prime
331 is prime
3331 is prime
33331 is prime
333331 is prime
3333331 is prime
33333331 is prime

But what about **333333331**

It turns out not to be, because:

$$17 \times 19607843 = 333333331$$

Which just goes to show that you can never trust a pattern just because it ***looks like*** it might continue. Mathematicians always need **proof**.

An unsolved mystery

The *mysterious* thing about primes is the way they seem to crop up at **random** among other numbers, without any pattern. Mathematicians have struggled for years to find a pattern, but with no luck. The lack of a pattern means prime numbers have to be hunted down, one by one.

HUNTING FOR PRIMES

	2	3	4	5	6	7	8	9	10
11	12	13	14	15	16	17	18	19	20
21	22	23	24	25	26	27	28	29	30
31	32	33	34	35	36	37	38	39	40
41	42	43	44	45	46	47	48	49	50
51	52	53	54	55	56	57	58	59	60
61	62	63	64	65	66	67	68	69	70
71	72	73	74	75	76	77	78	79	80
81	82	83	84	85	86	87	88	89	90
91	92	93	94	95	96	97	98	99	100

Small primes are easy to hunt by using a "sieve." To do this, write out the numbers up to 100 in a grid, leaving out the number 1 (which isn't prime). Cross out multiples of two, except for 2 itself. Then cross out multiples of 3, except for 3. You'll already have crossed out multiples of 4, so now cross out multiples of 5, then multiples of 7. All the numbers left in the grid (colored yellow above) will be prime.

2 **3** **5** **7** **11** **13** **17** **19** **23**

73939133 *is an amazing prime number. You can chop any number of digits off the end and still end up with a prime. It's the largest known prime with this property.*

The hunt for the biggest primes

A sieve is handy for finding small primes, but what about big ones? Is 523,367,890,103 a prime number? The only way to tell is to make sure nothing will divide into it, and that takes time. Even so, mathematicians have found some amazingly big prime numbers. The biggest so far is more than 7.8 million digits long. If you tried to write it in longhand, it would take 7 weeks to write and would stretch for 29 miles (46 km).

$100,000 REWARD

for the first person to find a prime number with more than ten million digits

The largest known prime number would fill 10 average books.

If you want to hunt for the biggest prime number, all you need do is download a program from the Web and let your computer do the rest. Worldwide, 40,000 people are doing exactly this. The first person to find a prime with more than 10 million digits will win a $100,000 prize.

Secret codes

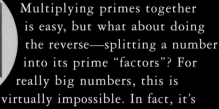

Multiplying primes together is easy, but what about doing the reverse—splitting a number into its prime "factors"? For really big numbers, this is virtually impossible. In fact, it's so difficult, it makes prime numbers perfect for creating unbreakable secret codes. When you spend money on the Internet, your details are hidden by a code made this way. The "lock" for the code is a huge number, and the "key" consists of the number's prime factors.

Prize numbers

Secret codes made from prime numbers are so reliable that one company in the US has offered a prize to anyone who can crack their code. If you can find the two prime numbers that multiply to give the number below, you'll win $20,000. Here's the number:

3107418240490004372135075003588856793003734602284272545720161948823206440518081504556346829671723 2867824379162728380334154710731085019195485290073377248227835257423864540146917366024776523466609.

Prime timing

Some insects use prime numbers for protection. Periodical cicadas spend exactly 13 or 17 years underground as larvae, sucking roots. Then they turn into adults, swarm out of the ground, and mate. Both 13 and 17 are prime numbers, so they can't be divided into smaller numbers. As a result, parasites or predators with a life-cycle of, say, two or three years almost never coincide with a swarm.

9 31 37 41 43

Pi

Draw a circle. Measure around it, then measure across. Divide the big number by the small one, and what do you get? The answer is 3 and a bit, or to be precise, pi. Humble pi, as it turns out, is one of the most remarkable numbers of all.

circumference

diameter

What is pi?

Pi is simply the *circumference* of a circle divided by the *diameter*. It works out the same for all circles, no matter how big they are. Test this for yourself with a piece of string. Use the string to measure the distance around cups, buckets, plates, and so on, and divide the length of the string by the distance across.

Pi is *impossible* to work out exactly

AN IRRATIONAL NUMBER

One of the weird things about pi is that you can't work it out exactly. There's no simple ratio, like 22 ÷ 7, that equals pi exactly. That makes pi an "irrational" number. If you wrote it out in full (which is impossible), its decimal places would continue forever.

3.141592

The HUNT for Pi

2000 BC
The Egyptians figured pi was $16^2/9^2$, which works out as 256/81, or 3.16. Not bad, but accurate to only one decimal place.

250 BC
Greek philosopher Archimedes drew 96-sided shapes around circles and so worked out that pi is between 220/70 and 223/71—accurate to 3 decimal places.

16th century
Ludolph van Ceulen worked out pi to 35 decimal places in Germany. But he died before the number was published, so it was carved on his gravestone

Pi can appear in surprising places. Think of a long, winding river that snakes across a flat plain to the sea, like the Amazon or the Mississippi. If you measure the length of the river and divide it by the distance as the crow flies from source to sea, the answer is close to pi. And not a circle in sight!

Every phone number in the *world* appears among the decimal places of pi

FOREVER AND EVER

As well as being infinitely long, pi's decimal places are totally random, with no mathematical pattern whatsoever. That means that the string of numbers contains, somewhere along it, every phone number in the world. And if you converted the numbers to letters, you'd find every book that's ever been written or will be written.

FAQ

What use is pi?

Pi is incredibly useful to scientists, engineers, and designers. Anything circular (like a can of beans) and anything that moves in circles (like a wheel or a planet) involves pi. Without pi, people wouldn't be able to build cars, understand how planets move, or figure out how many baked beans fit in a can.

Did you know?

In 1897, the state of Indiana tried to pass a law decreeing that pi is exactly 3.2. They wanted everyone in the world to use their value of pi and pay them a royalty, which would have earned millions. But just before the bill was passed, a mathematician pointed out that it was complete nonsense, and so the State Senate dropped it.

65358979323846264338327950288419716939925

1706 The English astronomer John Machin discovered a complicated formula for pi and used it to work out the first 100 decimal places.

1873 English mathematician William Shanks spent 15 years working out pi to 707 decimal places, but he made an error at the 528th decimal place and got all the rest wrong. Oops!

2004 Yasumasa Kanada in Tokyo worked out pi on a computer to 1.24 trillion decimal places.

FIND OUT MORE

The magic ones

By squaring numbers made of nothing but ones, you can make all the other digits appear. Even stranger, they appear in numbers that read the same forward and backward (palindromic numbers). The tiny twos below mean "times itself," or "squared."

$$1^2 = 1$$
$$11^2 = 121$$
$$111^2 = 12321$$
$$1111^2 = 1234321$$
$$11111^2 = 123454321$$
$$111111^2 = 12345654321$$
$$1111111^2 = 1234567654321$$

Do you think this pattern continues forever?

SQUARE *and*

When you multiply a number by itself, the answer is a *square number*. We call it square because you can arrange that many objects in a square shape. The square number series is one of the most important in math.

1   4   9   16

25   36

Prisoners' puzzle

Fifty prisoners are locked in cells in a dungeon. The prison guard, not realizing the doors are locked, passes each cell at bedtime and turns the key once. A second guard comes later and turns the locks in cells 2, 4, 6, 8, and so on, stopping only at multiples of 2. A third guard does the same, but stops at cells 3, 6, 9, 12, and so on, and a fourth guard turns the lock in cells 4, 8, 12, 16, and so on. This carries on until 50 guards have passed the cells and turned the locks, then all the guards go to bed. Which prisoners escape in the night?

Something odd

The first ten square numbers are 1, 4, 9, 16, 25, 36, 49, 64, 81, and 100. Work out the difference between each pair in the sequence and write your answers down in a row. Can you spot the pattern? The diagram on the right will help you see why this pattern happens.

1   3   5   7   9

what comes next: 1, 4, 9, 16, 25 ..?

Triangular NUMBERS

Take a pile of marbles and arrange them in triangles. Make each triangle one row bigger than the last, and count the number of marbles in each triangle. You'll end up with another special sequence: *triangular numbers*.

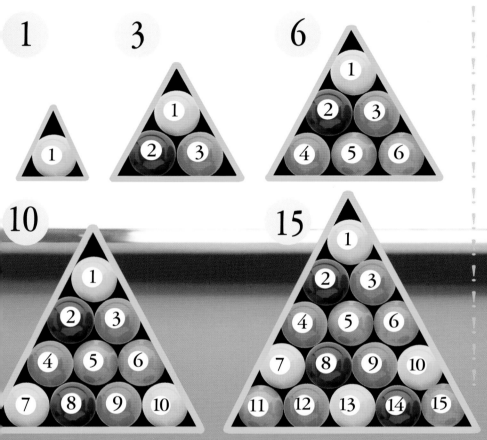

1

3

6

10

15

Squares from triangles

Triangular numbers are full of interesting patterns. Here's one of them: if you add neighboring triangular numbers together, they always make square numbers. Try it. Mathematicians can prove this mathematically using algebra, but there's an even simpler way to prove it, with pictures:

Adding up

A curious fact about triangular numbers is that you can make *any* whole number by adding no more than **three triangular numbers**. The number 51, for instance, is 15 + 36. See if you can work out which triangular numbers add up to your age. We know it always works because the rule was *proved* 200 years ago by one of the most brilliant mathematicians of all time: Karl Gauss.

Clever or just Gauss work?

Karl Gauss (1777–1855) was a mathematical genius. When he was a schoolboy, his teacher tried to keep the class quiet by telling them to add up every number from 1 to 100. But Gauss stood up within seconds with the right answer: 5050. How did he do it? Like most geniuses, he found a shortcut. He added the first and last numbers (1+100) to get 101. Then he added the second and second-to-last numbers (2+99) to get the same number, 101. He realized he could do this 50 times, so the answer had to be 50 × 101.

Did you know?

Triangular numbers never end in 2, 4, 7, or 9. Every other triangular number is a hexagonal number. If a group of *n* people shake hands with each other, the total number of handshakes is the (*n*−1)th triangular number.

what comes next: 1, 3, 6, 10, 15 ..?

Pascal's triangle

A good way to discover **patterns** in numbers is to make a "Pascal's Triangle"—a pyramid of numbers made by *adding*. Each number is the sum of the two numbers above. The triangle starts with a one at the top, so the numbers under this are both ones. Add these to make a two, and so on. You can add as many rows as you like.

What use i
Pascal's triangle

You can use Pascal's triangle to c
ways of combining things. Ima
you're buying an ice cream c
If there are 5 flavors, how n
combinations of flavor
possible? Count down 5
from the top (counting
top row as zero) for
answer: 1 way of ha
no flavors, 5 way
having 1 flavor,
ways of havi
flavors, 10 wa
having 3, 5
of having 4,
1 way of ha
all 5 flav

```
                    1
                 1     1
              1     2     1
           1     3     3     1
        1     4     6     4     1
     1     5    10    10     5     1
  1     6    15    20    15     6     1
1     7    21    35    35    21     7     1
1   8   28   56   70   56   28   8   1
1   9   36   84  126  126   84   36   9   1
1  10   45  120  210  252  210  120   45  10   1
1  11   55  165  330  462  462  330  165   55  11   1
```

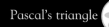

Chinese mathematicians knew about Pascal's triangle at least 900 years ago

Pascal's pinball

Pascal's triangle has links to two very important branches of math: probability and statistics. You can see why with a device called a Galton board, where marbles are poured through a pinball table with nails arranged like Pascal's triangle. The probability of a marble ending up in a particular column is easy to work out by looking at the numbers in Pascal's triangle. The final pattern is a shape called a bell curve—the most important graph in statistics.

Where are the *patterns?*

Pascal's triangle is full of fascinating number patterns. The most obvious one is in the second diagonal row on each side—the series of whole numbers. See if you can recognize the patterns below.

What number series is in the third diagonal? What series do you get if you add up pairs in this diagonal? *Hint: look back a page.*

```
            1
          1   1
        1   2   1
      1   3   3   1
    1   4   6   4   1
  1   5  10  10   5   1
1   6  15  20  15   6   1
1  7  21  35  35  21  7  1
1  8  28  56  70  56  28  8  1
1  9 36 84 126 126 84 36 9 1
1 10 45 120 210 252 210 120 45 10 1
1 11 55 165 330 462 462 330 165 55 11 1
```

Answer: the triangular and square numbers

Add up the numbers in each row. What series do the totals make? *Hint: look at the chessboard on page 37.*

```
            1
          1   1
        1   2   1
      1   3   3   1
    1   4   6   4   1
  1   5  10  10   5   1
1   6  15  20  15   6   1
1  7  21  35  35  21  7  1
1  8  28  56  70  56  28  8  1
1  9 36 84 126 126 84 36 9 1
1 10 45 120 210 252 210 120 45 10 1
1 11 55 165 330 462 462 330 165 55 11 1
```

Answer: powers of two

Add up the shallow diagonals, shown here as different colors. Do you recognize the series? *Hint: think of sunflowers and rabbits.*

1   2
3   5
8   13
?   ?
?
?

```
            1
          1   1
        1   2   1
      1   3   3   1
    1   4   6   4   1
  1   5  10  10   5   1
1   6  15  20  15   6   1
1  7  21  35  35  21  7  1
1  8  28  56  70  56  28  8  1
1  9 36 84 126 126 84 36 9 1
1 10 45 120 210 252 210 120 45 10 1
1 11 55 165 330 462 462 330 165 55 11 1
```

Answer: the Fibonacci series

THE ROAD FROM A TO B

Here's a puzzle you can solve with Pascal's triangle. Suppose you're a cab driver and want to drive from A to B in the city on the right. How many routes are possible? To help solve the puzzle, count the routes to nearby intersections and fill in the numbers.

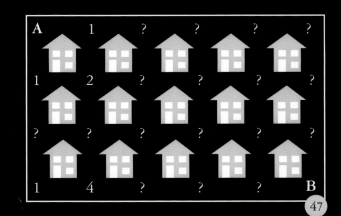

A	1	?	?	?	?
1	2	?	?	?	?
?	?	?	?	?	?
1	4	?	?	?	B

Mathe*magical*

Amaze your friends *and* family *with these*

Two wrongs make a right

When nobody's looking, take a sneaky peek at the top card in a deck (let's say it's the 10 of hearts). Announce that you will memorize the entire deck by flicking through them once. Give them a quick flick, then hand them to a friend. Ask your friend to *think of a number* from 1 to 10 and deal out that many cards, face down in a pile. Say the next card is the 10 of hearts and ask them to turn it over. It isn't, so pretend to be disappointed. Tell them to put it back and place the small pile back on top. Ask for another number between 10 and 20, then try again, pretending to be disappointed a second time. Finally, ask your friend to subtract the first number from the second, and try one last time. Now it works!

The amazing magic calculator

Give a friend a calculator and ask them to punch in any 3-figure number twice to make a 6-figure number. Tell your friend that the chance of 7 dividing into a random number without a remainder is 1 in 7. Ask them to try it. Any remainder? No. That was lucky! Tell them to try dividing the number on screen by 11. The chance of this working is 1 in 11. Any remainder? No—amazing! Now try dividing by 13. Any remainder? No—*astonishing*! To finish off, ask what's left. It's the original 3-figure number!!! But why?

The mind-boggling 1,089 trick

First do some preparation. Open a book on page 10, count down 8 lines and along 9 words. Write the 9th word on a slip of paper, seal it in an envelope, and place it on a table under the book. Now for the trick. Ask a friend to think of a 3-digit number and write it down. Any number will do as long as the first and last digits are different. Tell your friend to reverse the number and subtract the smaller one from the bigger one. For instance, 863 − 368 = 495. Then reverse the digits in the answer and add the two numbers: 495 + 594 = 1,089. Now tell your friend to use the first two digits in the answer as the page of the book. They should use the 3rd digit to find the line, and the last digit to find the word. Tell them to read the word out loud. Finally, ask your friend to open the envelope. This trick works because the answer is *always* 1,089!

Make someone
by magic

- Give a friend a calculator and tell them to key in the number of the month in which they were born
- Multiply by 4
- Add 13
- Multiply by 25
- Subtract 200
- Add the day of the month they were born
- Multiply by 2

tricks

mind-*boggling* magic tricks!

Secret sixes

Here's a game you can play with a friend and always win.
Ask a friend to tell you any number from 1 to 5. You then
choose a number from 1 to 5 and add them. Keep doing this
until one person wins by reaching 50. Here's how to make
sure you win. At the first chance you get, make the total
equal any of these numbers: **2, 8, 14, 20, 26, 32, 38, 44**.
So if your friend starts with 3, you add 5 to make 8. Now whatever
number they choose, you add the number that makes it up to 6 and the new
total will be 14. In this way, you're certain to be the one who reaches 50.

Magic dominoes

Ask a friend to choose a domino at
random from a set of dominoes, without
showing you the number. Now tell
them to multiply one of the two
numbers by 5, add 7, multiply by
2, and add the other number on
the domino. Ask for the final answer.

You can now work out what the domino is. Simply
subtract 14 from the answer to give you a two-digit
number made up of the two numbers on the domino.

ate of birth appear

calculator!

Subtract 40
Multiply by 50
Add the last two digits
of the year they were born
Subtract 10,500
Ask to look at the
calculator and then tell
them their full date of
birth. The *first* one or two
digits gives the month, the
next two gives the day, the
last two gives the year.

Impossible pairs

In this amazing trick you make a volunteer shuffle
a deck of cards, yet the cards magically arrange
themselves into pairs. First do some sneaky
preparation. Arrange the deck so that it's made of
alternating red and black cards. Now you're ready.
Ask a volunteer to cut the deck and do a "riffle
shuffle," using their thumbs to flick the two piles
together. It doesn't matter how badly they do the shuffle. Take the deck
back and briefly show the cards to the audience—they'll look random.
Now say you're going to split the deck at its "magic point." Look for
two cards the same color. Split the deck between them and bring the
bottom half to the top. Now comes the finale. Deal out the cards face
up in a pairs. Every pair will contain one red and one black card. This
trick works every time. Can you see why?

✪ SHAPING up

" Math is not just about numbers—it's much richer than that.

The ancient Greeks weren't especially good with numbers, but they were brilliant at math because they understood shapes. They used lines and angles to make shapes that helped them make sense of the world.

The Greeks invented the subject of geometry—the mathematics of shape and space. It's an area of math that helps us create and design anything from ballpoint pens to airliners. "

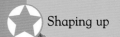
SHAPES *with*

THE RIGHT STUFF

Mathematicians' favorite triangles are those with one L-shaped corner: right-angled triangles.

Ancient Egyptians used right-angled triangles to make square corners to mark out fields or buildings. They knew a loop of rope with 12 equally spaced knots made a right angle if you **STRETCHED** it into a triangle with sides 3, 4, and 5 knots long.

The ancient Greeks knew about right-angled triangles, too. A man called **Pythagoras** discovered something special about them: if you draw squares on each side, the area of the two small squares adds up to the big square. It doesn't just work for squares, it works for any shape, even **elephants**!

So what? Pythagoras's discovery became the most famous math rule *of all time*. Pythagoras was apparently delighted with it—according to legend, he celebrated by sacrificing an ox.

Shapes made of straight lines are called **polygons**. The simplest polygons are triangles, which are made from three straight lines joined at three corners, or angles. Triangles are the building blocks for all other polygons.

Triangles can cover a flat surface *completely* without leaving gaps

No matter what shape a triangle is, the three angles always add up to 180°. Here's an ingenious way of proving it:

1 Use a ruler to draw a large triangle on a piece of paper. Then cut it out.

2 Tear off the three corners...

3 ...and put them together like this.

They'll always form a straight line, which proves the angles add up to 180°.

3 SIDES

SCALENE ISOSCELES EQUILATERAL OBTUSE RIGHT-ANGLED

Any shape made of straight lines can be split into triangles. Likewise, you can use triangles to create an endless variety of shapes. In China, people used this fact to invent a game called tangrams. The game reached the children of Europe and North America about 100 years ago, and caused a huge craze.

Triangles have special names depending on their sides and angles. If the sides are all equal, a triangle is *equilateral*. If the sides are all different, the triangle is *scalene*. If only two sides are the same, the triangle is *isosceles*. A triangle with one square side is *right-angled*, and one with an angle larger than 90° is *obtuse*.

Using just the 7 tangram pieces in the square on the left, you can make hundreds of different pictures.

Strong and simple

Triangles are the strongest of all simple shapes because, unlike squares and rectangles, their angles can't wobble. That's why you'll find triangles in bridges, buildings, and the girders of the Eiffel Tower in Paris.

height

angle

distance

How

do you measure the height of a tree without climbing it? Answer: use a right-angled triangle. As long as you know the size of one of the angles and one of the sides in a right-angled triangle, you can calculate the others. This branch of math goes by the scary name of *trigonometry*.

Different types

Squares and rectangles are the most obvious quadrilaterals, but there are others, too. Here are the 6 main types:

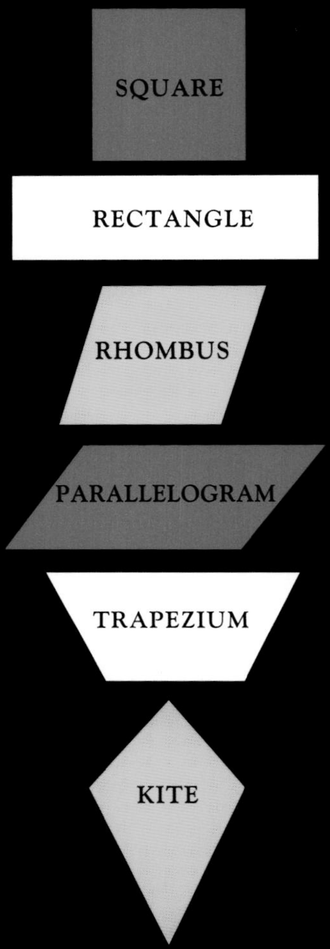

SQUARE

RECTANGLE

RHOMBUS

PARALLELOGRAM

TRAPEZIUM

KITE

SHAPES *with*

What do windows, walls, doors, the pages of this book, and millions of other human-made objects have in common? All of them are rectangles. Rectangles and other four-sided shapes are everywhere because they're easy to make and fit together neatly. Leave the book for a moment and look around you—how many can you count?

1 Draw a quadrilateral with a ruler. Cut it out and tear off all four corners.

2 Turn the corners around and see how they fit together.

Four angles

The four corners of a quadrilateral will always fit together perfectly, proving that the four corner angles always add to 360° (one whole revolution). If you remember from the previous page, a triangle's angles add up to 180°. So a quadrilateral is like two triangles added together.

PUZZLES

1

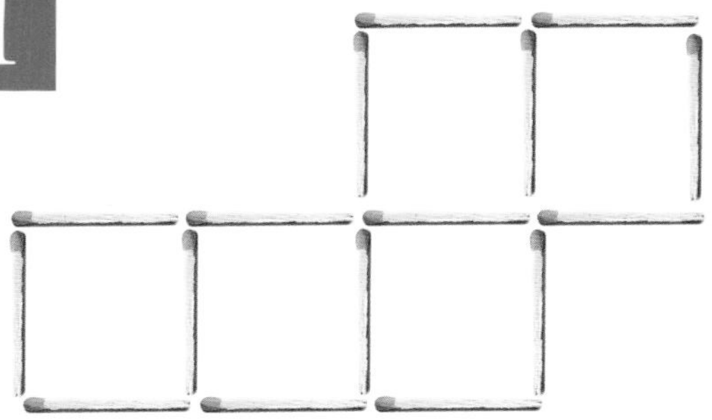

Arrange 16 matches in the pattern above. Can you figure out how to move *only two matches* so that there are four squares instead of five? You can't remove any matches and you can't leave any loose ends.

2 The owner of a **square house** wants to double the size of his home while still maintaining its square shape. There are four trees near the corners of the house, and the owner can't move them. He doesn't want to build a new story or a basement, so how can he do it?

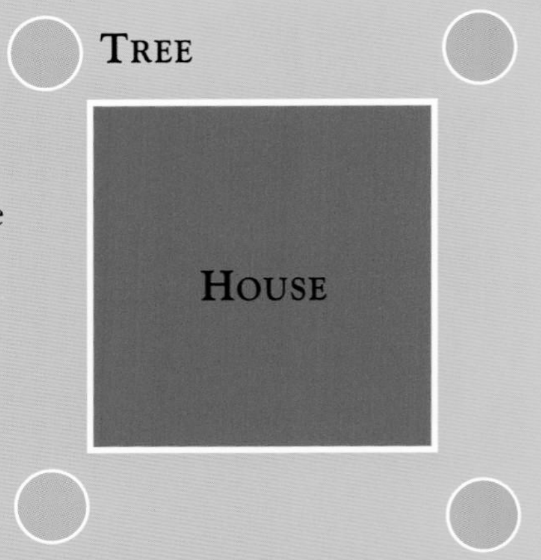

TREE

HOUSE

4 SIDES

... are called QUADRILATERALS

Shapes that fit

Shapes that fit together like tiles, without any gaps, are said to *tesselate*. The pictures below show that identical quadrilaterals always tesselate, whatever their shape. Triangles and hexagons also tesselate, but other polygons don't. So why do some shapes but not others tesselate? It all depends on the angles in the corners. If you can fit the corners together to make a full circle (360°) or a half-circle (180°), the shapes will tesselate.

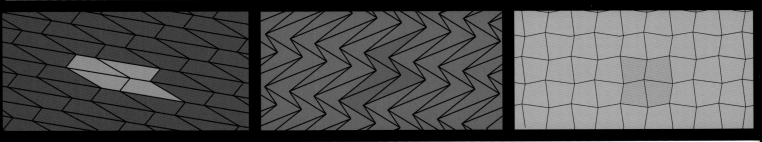

Do it yourself

You can **prove** that four-sided shapes always tesselate. Here's how. Use a ruler to draw *any* four-sided shape on a stack of about 12 pieces of newspaper. **Cut out** all 12 pieces at once (ask an adult to help if necessary). Use the cutouts to make a tiling pattern. You might find it tricky at first, so here's a hint: *start by lining up matching sides, but with the neighboring shapes pointing in opposite directions.*

3 Can you work out the length of the diagonal line in the picture below?

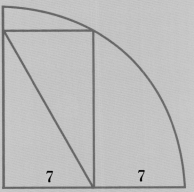

7   7

4 The square below has been divided into four identical pieces, and the L-shaped figure has also been dissected into four identical pieces. Can you dissect a square into *five identical pieces* (of some shape)?

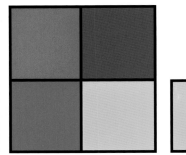

5 A plane needs to fly 140 miles from A to B, but there's a 50-mph wind blowing northeast. To allow for the wind, the pilot steers toward C, which is 100 miles away. If he heads toward C at 200 mph, when will he arrive at B?

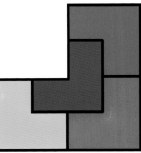

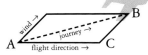

SHAPES
with many SIDES

Polygons with many sides have Greek names based on the number of sides. Pentagons and hexagons, which have 5 and 6 sides, are the most common. Shapes with many more sides are rare and have strange names like "11-gon" and "13-gon."

PENTAGON · HEXAGON · OCTAGON · NONAGON · DECAGON · 11-GON · DODECAGON · 13-GON

As the number of sides increases, polygons look more and more like circles. One way of describing a circle, therefore, is as a polygon with an *infinite* number of sides.

Nature's pentagons

Pentagons are rare in nature, but they do crop up in a few places. Cut an apple in half and look at the seeds — they're arranged in a ring of five. Starfish and sea urchins have bodies with five parts arranged in a ring.

Do pentagons fit together?

Pentagons won't tile a flat surface without gaps because their inner angles don't add up to 360°. However, you can use a mixture of pentagons and hexagons to tile a *curved*, 3D surface. Take a look at a soccer ball, and you'll see that's exactly how they're made.

Adding the angles

Here's a clever way to work out the inside angles of a **polygon**. The diagrams show a pentagon, but it works for any polygon. First think about the *outside* angles (labeled *a*). If you imagine the shape shrinking down to a dot, it's clear that the outside angles add up to a full circle, which is 360°. So each outside angle must be a fifth of this, which is 72°. Now for the *inside* angles (*b*). The first diagram shows that *a* and *b* make a half-circle, which is 180°. Since *a* = 72°, *b* must be 108°.

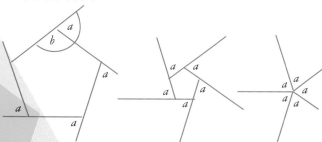

TO MAKE A PENTAGON, cut a strip of paper about 1 in (3 cm) wide and tie it in a knot. As you slowly flatten and tighten the knot, it will form a pentagon. When you hold it up to the light, you'll also see a 5-sided star (a pentagram)!

❶ ❷ ❸

Snow business

Hexagons are surprisingly common in nature. Snowflakes grow from hexagonal ice crystals, which is why they always have 6 arms—though every snowflake is slightly different. Bees store honey in a grid of hexagonal chambers called a honeycomb, and the eyes of insects are made of hexagonal lenses packed together. In some parts of the world, such as Giant's Causeway in Northern Ireland, you can even see hexagonal rocks.

Packing together

The main reason hexagons are common in nature is that they form naturally when circular objects pack together. Take a pile of coins of equal size and push them together until they're as tightly packed as possible. You'll see hexagonal rings just like the honeycomb in a beehive.

THINGS TO DO

Make a hexaflexagon

A hexaflexagon is an amazing paper toy that has 6 sides, 6 corners, 6 faces, and 6 colors. Each time you flex it, it folds in on itself and the color changes. With a bit of practice, you can make all 6 colors appear. Find out how to make one at the back of the book.

hexagons in nature

Magic mirrors

Draw a thick black line across a piece of white paper and stand two small mirrors over the line at right angles. (If you don't have mirrors, use CD cases with black paper inside so they reflect light.) Look in the mirrors and you'll see a square. If you change the angle of the mirrors, you can make a triangle, pentagon, hexagon, and other polygons magically appear!

The 3rd Dimension

TETRAHEDRON

CUBE

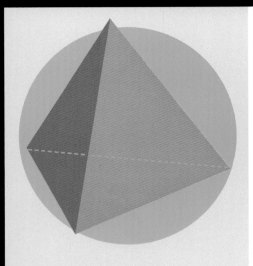

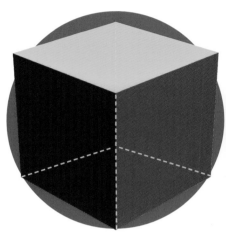

EULER'S RULE

One of the most brilliant mathematicians of all time was a German man named Leonhard Euler (his name is pronounced "oiler"). He wrote 75 books and was blind for the last 17 years of his life, yet he did half his best work then. One of his most famous discoveries concerned

Leonhard Euler (1707–1783)

the Platonic solids. Euler found that the number of faces, edges, and vertices (corners) in a 3-D shape obeys a simple mathematical rule. See if you can work it out. Fill in the table below by counting the number of faces, edges, and corners on each shape. Then look for a pattern. *Hint: for each shape, add the number of faces to the number of corners and compare the answer with the number of edges.*

	FACES	EDGES	CORNERS
CUBE	6	12	8
TETRAHEDRON	?	?	?
OCTAHEDRON	?	?	?
DODECAHEDRON	12	30	20
ICOSAHEDRON	?	30	12

• The tetrahedron is made of four equilateral triangles.
• The tetrahedron is a kind of pyramid, but unlike the famous pyramids of Egypt, its base is triangular rather than square.
• The ancient Greeks thought everything was made of four elements: earth, air, fire, and water. Because the tetrahedron has the sharpest corners of the Platonic solids, the Greeks thought fire was made of tetrahedral atoms.
• Because the tetrahedron is made of triangles, it is very strong. Diamond—the hardest substance known—is strong because its atoms are arranged in a grid of connected tetrahedrons.

• The cube is made of 6 squares joined at right angles.
• Cubes stack together more easily than any other shape. There's an infinite number of ways of stacking cubes together so they fit without any gaps.
• The Greeks chose the cube to represent the element earth, as cubes fit together so solidly. They thought rock might be made of cubic atoms.
• Some crystals, including table salt, grow naturally as cubes because the atoms within them are arranged in a cubic pattern.
• The four-dimensional version of a cube is a "hypercube." This shape can't exist in our universe, but mathematicians know it would have 32 edges, 16 corners, and 24 faces.

The ancient Greeks thought the *dodecahedron*

An infinite number of regular polygons can exist in two dimensions, but what if you try making perfectly regular shapes in 3-D, each with equal sides, angles, and faces? The ancient Greeks discovered that only five such shapes—called *Platonic solids*—are possible. They thought these perfect shapes were the invisible building blocks of the entire universe.

OCTAHEDRON DODECAHEDRON ICOSAHEDRON

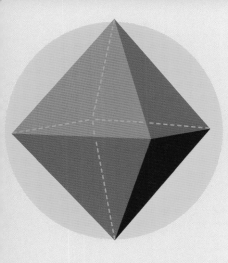

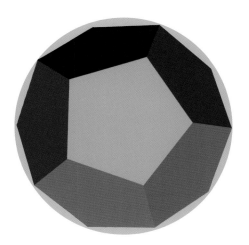

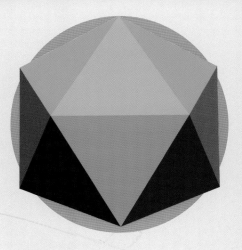

- The octahedron is made of 8 equilateral triangles arranged like two pyramids stuck together.
- Octahedrons, tetrahedrons, and cubes can all completely fill a space, without gaps.
- The Greeks saw the octahedron as being halfway between the tetrahedron (fire) and the cube (earth), so they decided it represented the element of air.
- The octahedron and cube are "dual shapes." If you chopped all the corners off an octahedron, you'd end up with a cube (and vice versa). If you slotted the two shapes together, the corners of each would stick through the midpoints of the other's faces.

- A dodecahedron is made of 12 pentagons. In Greek, "dodeca" means 2 + 10.
- The Greeks only needed four shapes for their theory about the elements, and the dodecahedron was the leftover. So as not to leave it out entirely, they decided that the dodecahedron was the shape of the entire universe, with its 12 faces corresponding to the 12 constellations of the zodiac.
- The dodecahedron and icosahedron are dual shapes, just as the cube and octahedron are. If you chopped the corners off a dodecahedron, you'd end up with an icosahedron (and vice versa).

- The icosahedron is made of 20 equilateral triangles.
- This shape represented the element of water to the Greeks. Perhaps they noticed that icosahedrons roll around easily, a bit like flowing water.
- The icosahedron has some surprising connections with nature. Some viruses (including chicken pox) and some microscopic sea creatures have bodies based on an icosahedron.
- If you slotted an icosahedron and dodecahedron together, the corners of each would stick through all the midpoints of the other shape's faces.

was the shape of the WHOLE UNIVERSE

Soccer balls and *buckyballs*

If you chop all the corners off an icosahedron, you end up with a shape made of 20 hexagons and 12 pentagons, just like a soccer ball. It's called a "truncated icosahedron." (Soccer balls always have 12 pentagons, but the other panels can vary in shape and number). In 1985, three scientists amazed the world when they discovered a chemical with exactly the same shape. Each molecule is a cage of 60 carbon atoms arranged in pentagons and hexagons. The discoverers called it the "buckyball" and won the Nobel Prize for finding it.

Dome homes

Truncated icosahedrons form the basic plan of super-strong buildings called geodesic domes. The frame of a geodesic dome consists of metal struts arranged in hexagons and pentagons. There can be any number of hexagons, but there are always 6 pentagons in a half-sphere. The hexagons and pentagons are split into triangles, which poke either inward or outward. The triangles make geodesic domes fantastically tough. They can withstand earthquakes, hurricanes, and burial under huge mounds of snow. There is even a geodesic dome on the South Pole, which has the worst weather on Earth.

THINGS TO DO

Here's an easy way to make a **TETRAHEDRON** from an envelope:

1 *fold*

Seal the envelope and fold it along the middle to make a faint crease.

2

Fold a corner to the center crease and make a mark with a pen where it meets.

3 *fold* *fold*

Cut across the mark. Then make two strong creases between the mark and the corners and fold them both ways.

4

Open out the tetrahedron and tape the hole shut.

To make an **ICOSAHEDRON,** cut out 3 pieces of posterboard, each 5 by 8¼ in (13 by 21 cm) in size. Make small notches in all the corners.

1

one like this

In each piece, cut a slot just over 5 in (13 cm) long in the middle. Ask an adult to help.

2

one like this

In one of the pieces, extend the slot all the way to one side.

3

Slot the pieces together and wind thread between the corners to make an icosahedron.

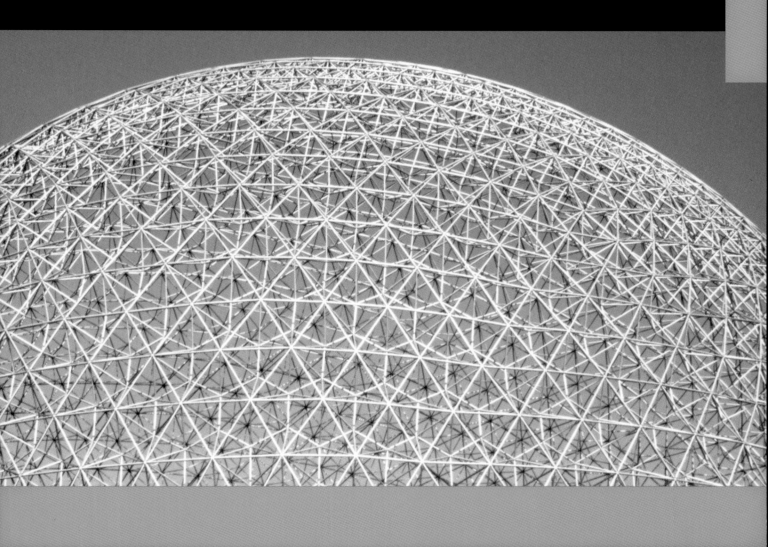

You can also make a super pop-up **DODECAHEDRON**:

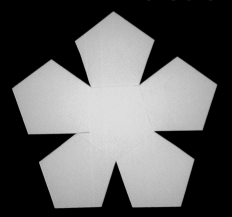

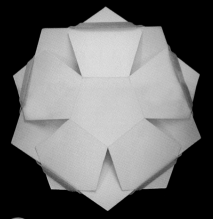

Cube puzzle

You can slice a cube into 27 smaller cubes if you make enough cuts. What is the minimum number of cuts needed to release the center cube? The answer is at the back of the book.

1 Photocopy the pattern above at double size and cut it out. Draw around it on stiff paper or cardboard, then redraw the lines with a long ruler. Cut it out and score around the middle pentagon to make creases. Then make a second copy.

2 Fold the side pentagons inward on each card to make a bowl shape. Hold these facing each other and weave a rubber band around the corners. If you let go, a dodecahedron will pop into shape!

Rolling coins

Place two coins side to side like this. (If possible, use coins with a milled edge.) Guess what position the head on the left coin will be in if you roll the coin around the top of the other one until it sits on the right. Try and see—you'll be surprised.

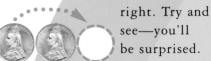

Bear hunter

A bear hunter leaves his camp and walks 5 miles due south. Then he turns left and walks 5 miles due east. He spots a bear, but it sees him and charges. He turns left again and run 5 miles due north, which takes him straight back to camp. What color was the bear?

Flying tonight

A woman is sitting crying in an airport lounge on Christmas Eve. A man walks past and sees her. "What's wrong?" he asks. "I've lost my plane ticket," she replies, "and now I can't get home for Christmas." "Don't worry," says the man, "I've got my own plane and can give you a ride. I'm going home for Christmas, too, and can drop you off on the way. It won't add anything to my journey." "But you don't know where I'm going," she replies. "I know," says the man. Where was he going?

Round and

Try drawing a circle by hand. It's tricky. If you can draw a very good circle, you might have a flair for art. But the way to draw *perfect* circles is by using a compass. What's more, compasses enable you to make magical designs and drawings.

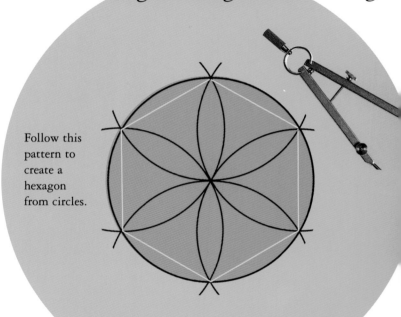

Follow this pattern to create a hexagon from circles.

SHAPES FROM CIRCLES

The ancient Greeks were fascinated by circles. They found that, by using just a compass and a straight edge (such as a ruler), you can construct lots of other shapes from circles, including hexagons and squares. Here's how to draw a hexagon. Use a compass to draw a circle. Put the point of the compass on the circle and draw a curve across it. Move the pin to the crossing point and repeat. Keep going until you've gone all the way around the circle, then use a ruler to draw between the crossing points.

A SLICE OF PI

The Greeks were also fascinated by pi—the ratio between the circumference (distance around) and the diameter (distance across) of a circle. Pi is impossible to measure exactly, but the Greeks had tried anyway, by comparing circles to other shapes ...

... here's a circle inside a square:

If the diameter is 1, the circumference must be pi. The distance around the square must be 4, since each side is 1. So pi is less than 4.

Here's a circle outside a hexagon:

The diameter is still 1 and the circumference is still pi. What about the distance around the hexagon? The radius of the circle is 0.5, so each side of the hexagon must be 0.5 long, too. That means the distance around the hexagon is 3. The circle is a bit bigger than the hexagon, so pi must be a bit more than 3.

The Greek mathematician Archimedes continued like this, getting closer to pi as he moved from hexagon to octagon and so on. He ended up drawing shapes with 96 sides and so proved that pi is between $^{223}/_{71}$ and $^{220}/_{70}$. And then he gave up.

DEATH BY MATH

According to legend, Archimedes was killed by a Roman soldier who lost his temper when Archimedes refused to stop drawing circles on the ground. Archimedes' proudest achievement was finding the formula for the volume and surface area of a sphere, which he found by studying wooden models of them. To honor this, he asked for a sphere and cylinder to be carved on his tomb.

Round

If you're a whiz at math, try this tricky puzzle: which is bigger in area—the blue ring on these pages or the three central rings (red, pink, and white combined)? Hint: the area of a circle is πr².

R.I.P.
MR. ARCHIMEDES
287–212 BC

A ROUND WORLD

Another clever Greek mathematician was Eratosthenes, who lived in Egypt around 1250 BC. He used circular math to prove Earth is round and even measured its size, which was amazing for a time when most people thought Earth was flat! So how did he do it?

Eratosthenes heard that at Syene (now Aswan) in southern Egypt, sunlight shone straight down wells in midsummer, when the sun was directly overhead. So, on the same day, he measured the angle of the sun in Alexandria in the north, and found it hit the ground at 7.2°, casting a small shadow. Eratosthenes realized this was because Earth was curved. Since the rays of sunlight are parallel, he also realized that two lines drawn straight to the center of Earth from these two places would meet at an angle of 7.2°. This is exactly a fiftieth of a circle (360°). So he just multiplied the distance between the two places—500 miles (800 km)—by 50 to get 25,000 miles (40,000 km) for the distance around Earth. It remained the most accurate estimate for 2,000 years.

Cones *and* curves

CUTTING CONES

An ancient Greek mathematician called Appolonius discovered that you can create the most important mathematical curves simply by cutting through a cone shape. The four most important types of curves are shown below.

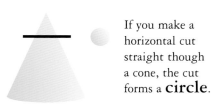

If you make a horizontal cut straight though a cone, the cut forms a **circle**.

Cutting across the cone at an angle produces a kind of oval called an **ellipse**.

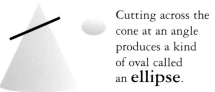

If you cut parallel to the side of the cone, the curve is a kind of arch called a **parabola**.

If you cut straight down through two cones placed tip to tip, you get twin curves—a pattern called a **hyperbola**.

Whenever you look at a circular object, you nearly always see it as an *ellipse*.

When you throw a ball, whether you throw it high or long, it will always fly in a curve called a *parabola* and arrive back on Earth. The parabola is just one of the math curves that the Greeks discovered and that scientists began to explore 400 years ago. These explorations led to one of the greatest discoveries of all time: that everything in the universe pulls on everything else through the mysterious force of *gravity*.

WHAT'S A PARABOLA?

When a football, a leaping dolphin, a waterfall, or a cannon ball flies through the air, it travels along a curved path. The great Italian scientist Galileo discovered this curve was a parabola. He realized that a cannon ball flies horizontally at a *constant speed* (allowing for air resistance), but the continuous pull of gravity makes it fall vertically at an *accelerating speed*. The result is a curve that gets steeper and steeper—a parabola.

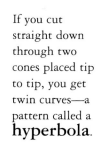

1   4

Why doesn't the

Galileo changed the world, for suddenly people stopped building city walls. For the first time, gunners could fire over walls and knew exactly where a cannon ball would land. A man called Kepler then found that planets revolve around the Sun in ellipses, and the genius scientist Isaac Newton saw that the Moon behaved in the same way as a cannon ball. So why doesn't the Moon fall to Earth?

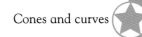

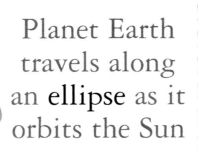

Planet Earth travels along an **ellipse** as it orbits the Sun

To draw an ellipse, loop a circle of string around two pins and pull the string with a pencil as you draw the curve.

WHAT'S AN ELLIPSE?

An ellipse looks like a squashed circle, but we can describe it more precisely by using math. Inside an ellipse are two points called foci. The ellipse is the line made by all the points whose combined distance from the two foci is the same. Many people think planets orbit the Sun in circles, but in fact they travel along ellipses. The Sun is at one of the two foci of each planet's orbit. The other focus is just empty space.

16

9

Galileo found a link between cannon balls and *square numbers*. Whatever distance the ball falls in the first unit of time, by the second it will have fallen *four times* as far, and by the third, *nine times* as far. So the distance the ball falls increases in ratio with the square of the time.

Moon fall into Earth?

Newton explained that the Moon is accelerating toward Earth, but it is going sideways precisely fast enough to keep it in orbit. By combining the work of Galileo and Kepler, Newton discovered how the force of gravity works.

FIND OUT MORE

Curves from lines

To prove his theory of gravity, Isaac Newton invented a new branch of math. He called it "fluxions," but we now call it calculus. Calculus is great for sums where something keeps changing, like the speed of an accelerating rocket. A graph would show this as a curve. By using calculus, we treat the curve as an infinite number of straight lines.

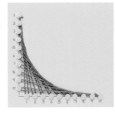

A cunning trick

The ancient Greeks didn't have calculus. Even so, Archimedes proved that the area under a parabola is two-thirds of the rectangle around it. How did he do it? He drew them on parchment, cut them out, and weighed them.

Useful parabolas

Parabolic mirrors reflect light to a point called a focus. Satellite dishes use this principle to collect faint signals from satellites and concentrate them onto a detector.

Radio telescopes use parabolic dishes to collect very faint signals from outer space.

SHAPES that STRETCH

3-D shapes can be topologically equivalent, too. A coin and a marble are topologically equivalent to each other, for instance, but neither is equivalent to a doughnut, which has a hole in the middle. However, a cup *is* equivalent to a doughnut, because both have a single hole going all the way through.

THE MÖBIUS STRIP

How many sides does a piece of paper have? Two, obviously. Is it possible for a piece of paper to have only one side? Yes, but it's a very strange piece of paper, invented by a mathematician called Möbius. This is how to make a Möbius strip.

① Neatly cut a long strip of paper. It should be at least 8 in (20 cm) long and at least 1 in (2.5 cm) wide.

half-twist *join*

② Make a half-twist and tape the ends togethe The paper now has only one side and one edge! Run a finger around it to check.

The four-color puzzle

What's the minimum number of colors you need to color in a map so that neighboring areas never have the same color? This puzzle, posed by Möbius in 1840, baffled everyone until it was solved in 1976 by a computer, which took 1,200 hours. Yet the puzzle seems simple. You can try the puzzle for yourself. Draw a continent and divide it into countries. Make the sea around it one color. Then see if you can color in all the countries around the coast in only three colors.

Topology is all about what happens to shapes when they stretch, twist,
and tangle. Some people call it *"rubber sheet"* geometry. If you can stretch and bend
a shape to make another, the two shapes are "topologically equivalent." A square and
a circle are topologically equivalent because you can stretch one to make the other.
But the figures 8 and 0 are not, because the 8 has a connection in the middle.

LOOK AT THESE SHAPES...

... and see if you can tell which of the objects
below are *topologically* equivalent
to them and which is in
a class of its
own.

3 Now for something very surprising. What do you think will happen if you cut all the way along the strip in the middle? Try it and see.

4 Make another Möbius strip. This time, cut along it a third of the way from the edge for another surprise.

Now make two circular ribbons of paper (not Möbius strips) and glue them together at one point. What shape do you think they will make if you cut along the middle of both ribbons?

And for my next trick...

Loop a strip of paper or a $10 bill into a zigzag and use two paperclips to hold it in shape. Ask a friend what they think will happen if you pull the ends. Give the ends a sharp tug and the paperclips will fly off, linked together! It's mathemagic!

A monk-y puzzle

Early one day, a monk set off to walk to a monastery at the top of a mountain. The path was steep, and it took him all day. The next day he returned down the same path, but set off much later and finished the walk in half the time. Was there any point where the monk was in exactly the same place at the same time on both days?

FIND OUT MORE

How symmetrical are you?

The human face is nearly symmetrical, but not quite. Put a mirror down a photo of your face to see how symmetrical you are. Look at the reflection of both halves—are they different? If you have a computer, try flipping each half of your face in turn to make two different pictures of your face.

It seems we get less symmetrical as we get older, with the left side of the face showing a bit more strain than the right side over the years. Check your parents' faces and see if they're less symmetrical than your own.

The real you

If you want to see what you *really* look like, you need to use two mirrors rather than one. Position them at right angles and then look into the corner. What happens when you move your head to the left or right? The image you see is not reversed but the real you—just as everyone else sees you! Scary, huh?

Shapes with lateral symmetry repeat themselves when you flip them

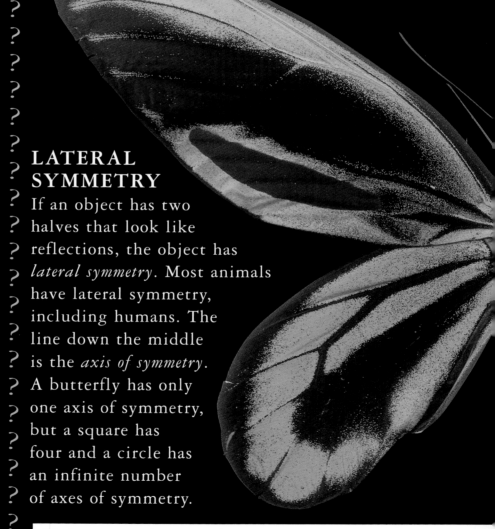

LATERAL SYMMETRY

If an object has two halves that look like reflections, the object has *lateral symmetry*. Most animals have lateral symmetry, including humans. The line down the middle is the *axis of symmetry*. A butterfly has only one axis of symmetry, but a square has four and a circle has an infinite number of axes of symmetry.

HOW MANY AXES OF SYMMETRY

ЯOЯЯIM

Shapes with rotational symmetry repeat themselves if you rotate them

Are starfish symmetrical?

A starfish has five axes of lateral symmetry. It also has what mathematicians call *rotational symmetry*, which means you see the same shape repeated if you turn the object around while keeping the center point still. A parallelogram and the letters N, S, and Z all have rotational symmetry but not lateral symmetry.

Leonardo da Vinci *wrote everything* in mirror writing

Why do mirrors flip the world?

Why does a mirror swap left and right but not top and bottom? In fact, a mirror doesn't really swap left and right at all. If you stand in front of a mirror and wave your left hand, the hand that waves back is still on the left. It isn't a reflection of your right hand, it's your *apparent* left hand opposite your *actual* left hand, just as your apparent head is opposite your actual head. The confusion happens because we imagine ourselves standing behind the mirror. Try holding a 90° mirror (bottom left) sideways—wow! Now you're upside down!

DO THE OBJECTS BELOW HAVE?

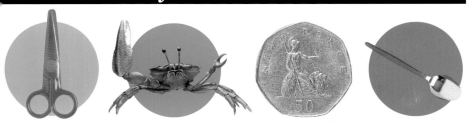

THINGS TO DO

Mirror writing

Hold some paper on your forehead and write your name on it. Many people write a reflection of their name when they do this, even though mirror writing is normally difficult. The artist Leonardo da Vinci always wrote in mirror writing so that his secret notes were difficult to read.

Make a paper chain

To make a chain of symmetrical figures, fold a long strip of paper in a zigzag and draw half the red man on top, making sure arms and legs extend to the edge. Cut through all the layers and open out the chain.

Palindromes

Sentences that read the same forward or backward are called palindromes. "Madam I'm Adam" is a palindrome. Numbers can also be palindromes, and there's a clever way to make them. Take any number with more than one digit, reverse it, then add the two numbers. If you don't get a palindrome the first time, repeat the process. Most numbers only take a few steps to make a palindrome, but the numbers 89 and 98 take 24 steps each. Oddly, it's impossible to make a palindrome from 196.

Amazing

The mathematician *Leonhard Euler* founded network theory by studying the math of mazes

MAZES

TYPES OF MAZES

Simple mazes

Most mazes are easy to solve just by keeping your left (or right) hand on one wall along the way. Try this on the maze below, from Hampton Court in England.

Complex mazes

In a complex maze, the center is surrounded by walls that aren't connected to the rest of the maze, so the one-hand rule doesn't work. Below are two mazes in one. Find your way to the center, then out through the other exit.

To a mathematician, a maze is a topological puzzle. Usually, the more unconnected walls there are, the harder the maze is. The maze below was set up in the garden of English mathematician W. W. Rouse Ball more than 100 years ago. It's a tricky one, and you can't solve it with the one-hand rule. To find your way through, look for dead ends and color them in.

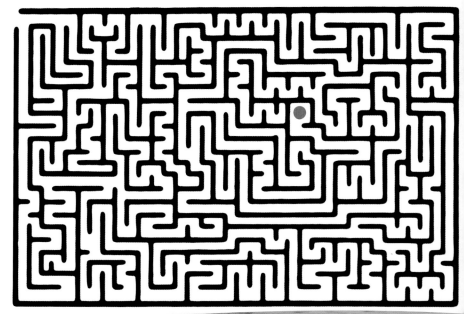

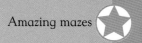

MAKE A MAZE

This simple maze design has been found at ancient sites all over the world, from Finland to Peru. It's very easy to draw one yourself, starting with a cross.

1 Draw a cross and 5 dots as shown here. Make a loop from the top of the cross to the upper left dot.

2 Draw a second loop from the upper right dot to the right side of the cross.

3 The third loop starts on the left of the cross and ends at the dot below it. Keep this loop wide.

4 The final loop starts at the lower right dot and ends at the bottom of the cross.

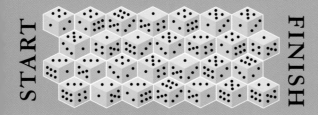

START **FINISH**

On a normal die, the opposite faces always add up to seven. In the dice maze on the left, some of the dice must be faulty. See if you can find your way across the maze by stepping only on dice that don't add up.

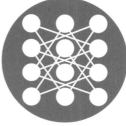

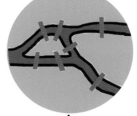

Are the pink dots inside or outside this spiral maze? Can you work out the mathematical rule that tells you whether a dot is inside or outside the maze?

The dark blue stick in the picture above is lying on top of all the other sticks. If you picked off the top sticks one by one, what order would they come off in?

Can you find a route through the maze above that visits every circle once only? Here's a hint: start in the middle of the top row and end in the middle of the bottom row.

The Russian town of Königsberg had seven bridges and two islands. The local people found they could not take a walk that crossed each bridge once only. Leonhard Euler explained why, and that was the start of a branch of math called "network theory" Try it. Can you explain why it's impossible?

PUZZLING *SHAPES*

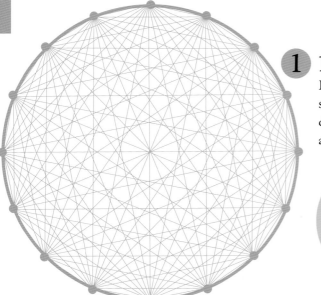

1 Divided circles

If you draw three dots on a circle and connect them all with straight lines, the circle is divided into 4 areas. Four connected dots divide the circle into 8 areas, and 5 dots divide it into 16 areas. How many areas will 6 connected dots create? *Clue: not 32!*

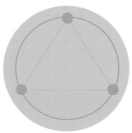 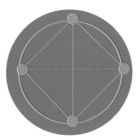 

2 Alphabet puzzle

Why are some of these letters above the line and others below it? *Clue: you don't need numbers to solve this puzzle.*

AEFHIKLMNTVWXYZ
- -
BCDGJOPQRSU

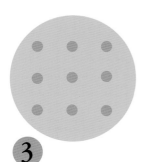    

3 How can you connect all 9 dots above with only 4 straight lines?

4 How can you cut a cake into 8 equal pieces by making only 3 straight cuts?

5 How can you cut a doughnut into 12 pieces with only 3 straight cuts?

6 How is it possible to push a large doughnut through a cup handle?

7 How can you plant 10 rose bushes in five straight rows, each with 4 bushes.

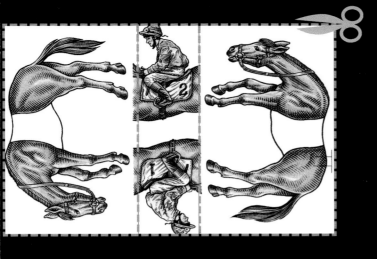

⑧ Horses and riders

Trace or photocopy this drawing, then cut along the dotted lines to make three pieces. How can you arrange the pieces so that each rider is correctly riding a horse, without folding or cutting any of the pieces?

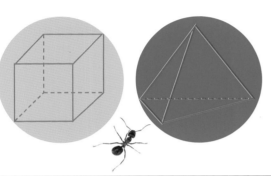

⑨ The exploring ant

Imagine an ant walking around these shapes. Can it walk along all the edges of each shape without retracing its path? To find out, try drawing each shape as one line, without lifting your pen. Can you work out the rule that determines which shapes the ant can walk around?

⑩ Sliding coins

Arrange six coins in a parallelogram. How can you change the shape into a circle by moving only 3 coins? You can't nudge coins aside, and each coin you move must end up touching two others.

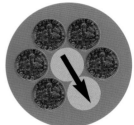

The move above is forbidden because you're not allowed to nudge coins out of the way.

⑪ Colored cubes

A cube has been painted so that each of its six faces is a different color. The three pictures here show it in different positions. Which color is face down in the third picture? *Clue: try turning the cube around in your mind.*

⑫ Through the paper

By cutting along a clever pattern, it's possible to make a hole in a postcard-sized piece of paper that a person can step through. Can you work out the pattern?

123 The world of MATH

The great Italian
scientist Galileo once said,

"everything in the universe
is written in the language
of mathematics."

Sure enough, math has helped
us unravel many of the universe's
secrets. And in doing so, it has
driven civilization forward.

As our understanding of the
world progressed, people had to
invent new and different types of
math. Math grew bigger and better,
with ever more branches. Now
mathematical ideas help us
understand every aspect of the world,
from card games to the weather,
from art to philosophy.

FIND OUT MORE

The best bet

Ever wondered why casinos make so much money? The answer is that they make sure the odds are stacked against you. Look for the green zero on a roulette wheel. When the ball lands there, nobody wins. You have a 1 in 37 chance of winning on a number, but the casino only pays 36 times your bet. So on average, they always win.

Pi sticks

There's an interesting link between probability and pi (π). Drop matchsticks on a grid of lines one matchstick apart. The chance of a match touching a line is $2/\pi$, or about 0.64. Below, of 22 matches, around 14 should lie on a line (since $0.64 \times 22 = 14$). Try it for yourself.

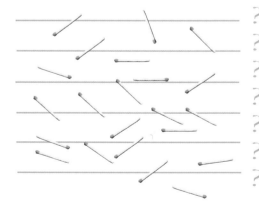

TAKE A

What's the chance of being **struck by lightning** or hit by a meteorite when you go for a walk? If you fly in a plane, what's the chance of crashing or seeing a flying pig though a window? To answer these questions precisely, you need a branch of math called probability.

WHAT IS PROBABILITY?

Probability is expressed by a number from zero to one. A probability of *zero* means something definitely won't happen, whereas a probability of *one* means it definitely will. Anything in between means something *may* happen. For instance, the chance of a coin landing heads up is a half, or 0.5.

MENDEL'S NUMBERS

In the 1850s, Austrian monk Gregor Mendel made an amazing discovery thanks to probability. Mendel bred purple-flowered peas with white-flowered peas and found that all the offspring were purple. He decided these must have "white" in them, but it just wasn't showing. So he bred the offspring with each other. Now there were four possibilities. The new parents could pass on one purple each, a purple and a white, a white and a purple, or two whites. If purple was present, it would show over white, and so on average, only a quarter of the plants would be white. They were. Mendel had discovered genes.

P/P	w/w

P/w	P/w	P/w	P/w

P/P	P/w	P/w	w/w

CHANCE

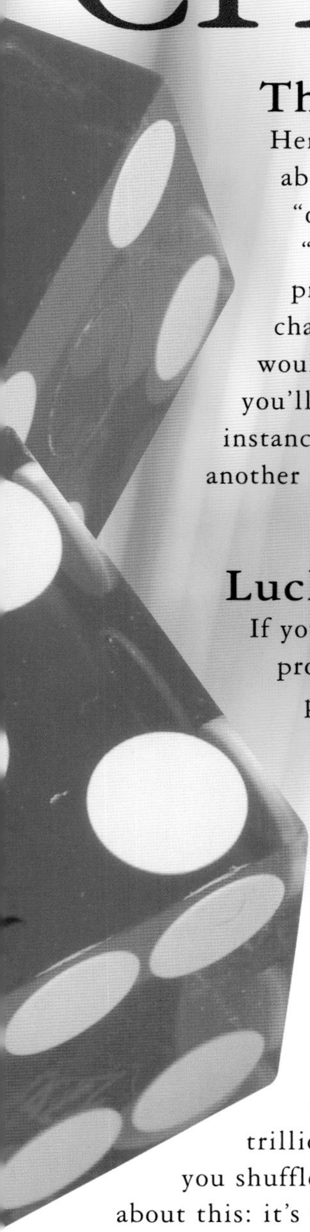

The laws of luck

Here's a handy tip. In math questions about probability, look for the words "or" and "and." When you see the word "or," chances are you'll need to **add up** probabilities to get your answer. So the chance of rolling a one *or* a two with a die would be ⅙ + ⅙ = ⅓. When you see "and," you'll probably have to **multiply**. For instance, the chance of getting a six *and* another six on two dice rolls is ⅙ × ⅙ = ¹⁄₃₆.

Luck of the draw

If you shuffle a deck of cards, what's the probability that the cards will end up in one particular order? The answer is 1 over the total number of card combinations possible. We can work out the total number of card combinations like this:

$$52 \times 51 \times 50 \times 49 \times .... \times 1$$

(We write the sum in shorthand as 52!) This sum produces a **very** big number: *80 million trillion trillion trillion trillion trillion*. So the chance that your cards are in one particular order is 1 in 80 million trillion trillion trillion trillion trillion. Next time you shuffle a pack of cards, think about this: it's very likely that nobody in the history of the universe has ever had exactly the same order of cards before!

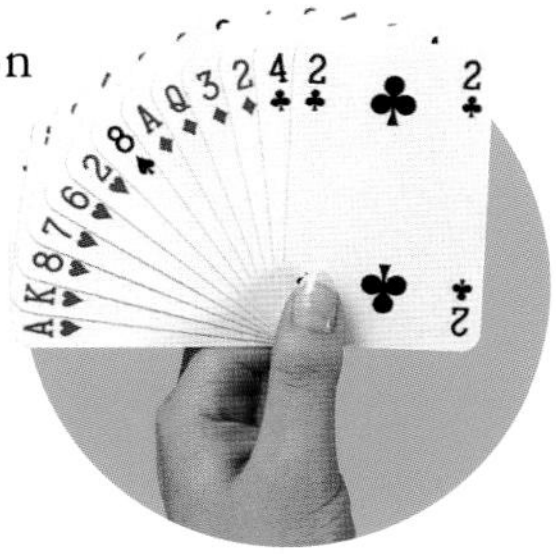

RISKY BUSINESS

Some people are terrified of lightning but happy to smoke. If they understood probability, they might think differently. The table shows your chance of dying from various causes, based on death rates in Europe and North America.

CAUSE OF DEATH	CHANCE OF DYING IN A YEAR
 smoking 10 cigarettes a day	1 in 200
 heart attack	1 in 300
 road accident	1 in 4,000
 flu	1 in 5,000
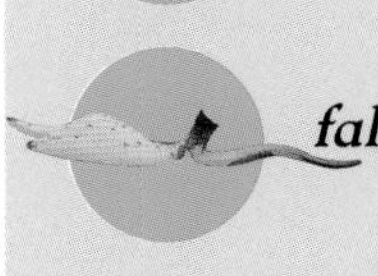 falling	1 in 16,000
 playing soccer	1 in 25,000
 murder	1 in 100,000
 struck by lightning	1 in 10 million
 hit by meteorite (estimate)	1 in a trillion

SNEAKY SPINNERS

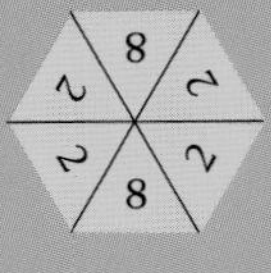

Here's a game of chance you'll keep winning at. Make four spinners like the ones here by cutting out cardboard hexagons and writing numbers on them. Push a toothpick through the center of each. Then challenge a friend to a spinner match. Point out that they can choose any spinner they want, and the

numbers on each one add up to 24, so the game must be fair. Look at the highest number on their spinner, then make sure you pick the spinner with the next number up (but if your friend takes the one with an 8 on it, you take the one with a 5 on it). You'll have a two-thirds chance of winning each match!

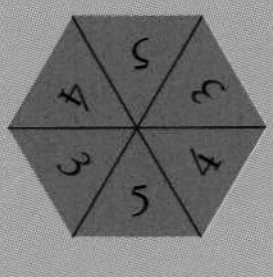

A butterfly beating its wings in

ChaOs
The math of messes

Some things are easy to predict using a bit of math. We know exactly where the planets will be in 100 years and how high the tide will rise next Christmas, for instance. Other things are nigh on impossible to predict, like where a pinball will go or what the weather will be like in a week.

The reason is a mathematical phenomenon called *chaos*.

HURRICANE WARNING

What is chaos?

If something is chaotic, a tiny change in the starting conditions has a huge impact on the final outcome. Pinball makes use of chaos. Each ball you fire takes a different route. Tiny differences in the ball's starting position or the amount you pull the spring become magnified into major changes in direction as it bounces around the table.

Over billions of years, the motion of Earth and the

Brazil can trigger a tornado in Texas

Make a chaos pendulum

A pendulum is a weight that swings back and forth on a length of string. Ordinary pendulums are predictable, but you can make a totally unpredictable "chaos pendulum" by using magnets. Use a bar magnet as the weight and suspend this over a table. Fix three more magnets to the table below, making sure the pendulum can't touch them. Swing the weight and watch what happens.

START A HURRICANE

Weather works a bit like pinball. When forecasters try to predict the weather, they find that tiny differences in the starting conditions lead to totally different outcomes after 4–5 days. We call it the butterfly effect, because it means that a butterfly beating its wings in Brazil could, in theory, cause a tornado in Texas. You can do exactly the same thing—if you blink, you might cause a hurricane in Hawaii or a typhoon in Taiwan!

Chaos in the bathroom

You can see chaos with your own eyes by slowly turning on a faucet. First it drips. Open it a bit more. Now a smooth, steady trickle comes out. Open it a bit more and the trickle gets messy—it gurgles, twists, and splashes. The flow has become "turbulent," which means its motion is chaotic. A similar thing happens when you put a candle out. A smooth stream of smoke rises predictably for a few inches, then it suddenly turns chaotic, swirling and rippling in complicated patterns.

other planets through space is as chaotic as pinball

Freaky FRACTALS

Until about 100 years ago, mathematicians only studied *perfect* shapes like triangles and circles. But such shapes are rare in the real world. In nature, shapes are messy— think of a **wiggly coastline** or a **jagged mountain**. Unlike a circle, which gets smoother and flatter when you magnify it, a mountain stays just as jagged because you see ever more detail as you get closer. In 1975, mathematician Benoit Mandelbrot gave these *endlessly intricate* shapes a name. He called them **fractals**.

Mandelbrot set

Mandelbrot created amazing fractal patterns on his computer by generating graphs with what mathematicians call "imaginary numbers." The most famous, called the Mandelbrot set, is said to be the most complex object in mathematics. It gets ever more detailed and beautiful when you zoom in and enlarge tiny portions of it, and the detail continues forever. Even stranger, the same basic shapes appear again and again, though with infinite variations.

Fractal broccoli

A fractal made of small copies of itself is said to be "self-similar." Broccoli and cauliflower are self-similar fractals because the florets (and the tiny florets on them) are the same shape as the whole vegetable. Romanesco broccoli even looks a bit like the Mandelbrot set.

Koch's snowflake

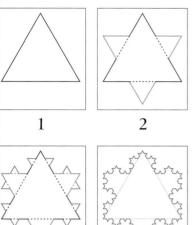

Draw an equilateral triangle, then draw small equilateral triangles a third as wide on its sides. Do the same again, and continue doing this forever. The result is a fractal called "Koch's snowflake"—a curved line made purely of corners. This mind-boggling fractal has an infinitely long perimeter but a finite area.

Triangles in triangles in triangles

Another simple way to make a fractal is to draw triangles inside triangles and keep doing this forever. This fractal is called "Sierpinski's gasket." Amazingly, if you color in multiples of 2 or 3 in Pascal's triangle, you'll see a very similar pattern take shape.

Crinkly coastlines

How long is the coastline of North America? It's impossible to give a simple answer to this question because a coast is a fractal line. If you measured it on an atlas, you'd get one answer. If you used a more detailed map, you'd discover more wrinkles and would get a bigger answer. And if you drove or walked along the coast, you'd get a bigger answer still. The rate by which these measures increase as you zoom in is called the *fractal dimension*.

Ice ferns

Some of the most common natural fractals form when something branches over and over again, like a tree trunk splitting into boughs, branches, and twigs. We call this pattern "dendritic." Frost ferns, rivers and tributaries, and the veins in your body all make dendritic fractals.

FIND OUT MORE

Using logic

Sometimes it's quicker to solve a puzzle by thinking than by trying it out. Here's an example. Imagine a chessboard has two opposite corners missing. Can you cover the remaining 62 squares with only 31 dominoes, each domino covering two squares? You could try to solve the puzzle by placing dominoes in different patterns, but this could take forever. With logic, you can solve it in seconds. *Hint: what color are the two missing squares? So?*

What's a paradox?

A paradox is a statement that seems to contradict itself when you think about it logically. Imagine you're walking toward the North Pole, with a compass showing north ahead and west on your left. If you walk across the pole and then turn around, west switches over to the other side. It seems impossible, but it's true. Here's another. A barber in a village shaves everyone who doesn't shave himself. Who shaves the barber? Turn to the back of the book for the answer.

LOGIC

This branch of math relies on **thought** rather than numbers or shapes. Given a starting point, if you can **deduce** certain things, and then link your deductions together until you have a solution, then you have solved the problem **logically**.

Logic puzzles

DEATH ROW

A judge is sentencing a prisoner guilty of a heinous crime. He tells the prisoner that because the crime is so bad, he will be hanged at noon within a week, but to make his suffering worse, he will not know the day of the execution until that day arrives. The prisoner thinks for a few seconds and then says, laughing, "but that means I can't be hanged." How does he know?

THE TIGER

A mother and her son are working in the field in India. A tiger leaps out of the long grass and pins the boy to the ground with his claws. "Let him go!" cries the woman. "I will," says the tiger (it was a talking tiger), "provided you can correctly predict the fate of your child—either that I eat him or that I let him go." What should the woman predict?

"I think, therefore I am"

The French mathematician René Descartes (1596–1650) used logic to prove that there was only one thing he could be completely sure of—his own existence. He summed it up in Latin: *Cogito, ergo sum* ("I think, therefore I am"). Descartes' main claim to fame was the invention of Cartesian coordinates. He's less well known for doing all his greatest work in bed.

THREE DOORS

You're on a TV game show. The host shows you three closed doors and tells you there's a shiny black sports car behind one of them. If you choose the right door, you win it. You pick a door at random. The host, who knows where the car is, then opens another door and shows you an empty room. He asks if you want to change your mind. Should you?

THREE HATS

Three sisters, A, B, and C, are wearing hats, which they know are either black or white but not all are white. A can see the hats of B and C; B can see the hats of A and C; C is blindfolded. Each is asked in turn if they know the color of their own hat. The answers are: A: "No." B: "No." C: "Yes." What color is C's hat and how does she know?

ZENO'S PARADOX

A Greek philosopher called Zeno thought up a paradox involving the idea of infinity. A man called Achilles challenges a tortoise to a race. Suppose Achilles can run ten times faster than the tortoise, but he gives the tortoise a 10-meter head-start. When Achilles has run 10 meters, the tortoise has run 1 meter and is still in the lead. When Achilles has covered that 1 meter, the tortoise has moved another tenth of a meter forward. Each time Achilles tries to catch up, the tortoise has gone a bit farther still. This can continue forever, the tortoise moving forward by ever smaller increments. So it seems logical that Achilles can never overtake the tortoise—yet common sense tells us that anyone can overtake a tortoise in a race!

The puzzle baffled the Greeks because they didn't understand the idea of infinity. They thought an infinite number of values, however tiny, must add up to an infinite amount. The problem wasn't fully solved until the 1600s, when a Scottish mathematician, James Gregory, showed than an infinite number of ever-decreasing values can add up to a *finite* amount.

The ART of *math*

Vanishing point

Vanishing points

During a period of history called the Renaissance, artists started using math to make pictures look more 3-D. They realized that distant objects should be small, and that lines receding into the distance should converge at one place—the "vanishing point." In the painting above by Carpaccio (1514), the vanishing point is to the right of the canvas.

Artists use math

The Dutch illustrator M.C. Escher created impossible, dreamlike worlds by deliberately breaking the mathematical rules that artists use to make pictures look 3-D. He used symmetry, tesselation, and the concept of infinity everywhere in his art, making him the most fascinating mathematical artist ever.

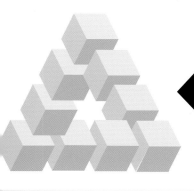

Just an illusion

This mind-bending shape is called a Penrose triangle. The pattern of shade tricks the human brain into seeing a 3-D triangle, each corner of which is 90° (a right angle)—a mathematical impossibility.

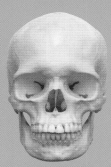

Can you find two skulls hidden in the painting on the left?

A hidden skull

"The Ambassadors" (1533) by Hans Holbein has a peculiar smear at the bottom. If you hold the page close to your eye and look at the smear from lower left or upper right, you'll see it's a skull. Holbein used perspective geometry to draw this skull, but its meaning is a mystery. There is also a second, much tinier, skull on one of the men's caps.

3-D art

These days, people use computers to create 3-D images. The picture above is a stereogram. If you look through it and move it slowly forward or back, you'll see candies magically floating in midair.

o create optical effects,

such as the *illusion* of three dimensions

Escher's "House of Stairs" looks impossible because he gave it two vanishing points and made parallel lines run toward and around them in curves. Each of the creatures (which Escher called "curl-ups") belongs to one vanishing point or the other. The top of the picture is a repetition of the bottom, so the scene might conceivably carry on forever

In Escher's "Circle Limit IV," angels and demons form a tesselating pattern, with the spaces between one cleverly forming the shapes of the other. The pattern shrinks toward the edge, seeming to continue to infinity. Escher created this picture to represent an impossible 2-D surface that mathematicians call a hyperbolic plane.

MATH TOP tips

The secret to becoming a **genius** at math is to use shortcuts. All math experts do this, from brilliant scientists to quick-thinking tradesmen. Some of the best tricks are shown on this page. When you've practiced using them, you can work out complicated problems in your head without even touching a calculator.

STAIRWAY TO ELEVEN

Multiplying by 11 is easy if you remember that 11 is ten plus one. To multiply 63 by 11, simply multiply by 10 (to give you 630) and add 63 once, giving you 693.

ROUNDING OFF

ADDING TOGETHER LARGE NUMBERS IN YOUR HEAD IS OFTEN EASIER IF YOU ROUND OFF ONE OF THE NUMBERS TO THE NEAREST 10. For instance, to add 46 and 39, round off the 39 to 40 by adding 1.
So, 46 + 40 = 86. To finish off, subtract the 1 you added, to make 85.

HIGH FIVES

DIVIDING OR MULTIPLYING BY 5 MUCH EASIER IF YOU REMEMBER THAT FIVE IS HALF OF TEN. For example, to work out 5 × 36, first work out 10 × 36, which is 360. Then halve this for the final answer: 180. To divide a large number by 5, divide it by ten first and then double the answer. So, to find out 325 ÷ 5, work out 325 ÷ 10 = 32.5. DOUBLING THIS GIVES YOU 65.

Short division

MAGIC NUMBER TRICK

There are several tricks that tell you whether a number is divisible by 3, 4, 5, 9, 10, 11. ÷

✳ To find out if a NUMBER is divisible by 3, add up the digits. If they add up to a MULTIPLE of 3, the number is divisible by 3. For instance, 192 must be divisible by 3 because $1 + 9 + 2 = 12.$

✳ A number is DIVISIBLE by 4 if the last two digits are 00 or a multiple of 4.

✳ A number is divisible by 5 if the LAST DIGIT is 5 or 0.

✳ A number is divisible by 9 if all the digits add up to a MULTIPLE of 9. FOR INSTANCE, 201,915 must be divisible by 9 because $2 + 0 + 1 + 9 + 1 + 5 = 18.$

✳ A numbers is DIVISIBLE by 10 IF THE LAST DIGIT is 0.

✳ TO FIND OUT IF A NUMBER IS DIVISIBLE BY 11, START WITH THE DIGIT ON THE LEFT, subtract the next digit from it, add the next, subtract the next, and so on. IF THE ANSWER is 0 or 11, then the original number is divisible by 11. For instance, is 35706 divisible by 11? $3 - 5 + 7 - 0 + 6 = 11$, so the answer is **yes**.

1 First write down the number nine (as a word) on a piece of paper and seal it in an envelope.

2 Give the envelope to a friend and tell them to keep it safe.

3 Next give your friend a calculator. Ask them to key in the last two numbers of their phone number.

4 Add the number of dollars in their pocket.

5 Add their age.

6 Add the number of their house.

7 Subtract the number of brothers and sisters they have.

8 Subtract 12.

9 Ask them to add their favorite number.

10 Multiply the answer by 18.

11 Ask them to add up all the digits in the answer.

12 If the answer is more than 1 digit long, ask them to add up the digits again. Keep going until there's only one digit, which will be 9.

13 Finally, tell your friend to open the envelope and read out the number.

Who's who?

The brilliant scientist and mathematician Isaac Newton once said, "If I have seen farther, it was by standing on the shoulders of giants." Newton meant that his own work, like that of all mathematicians, was built on the work of the great mathematicians who lived before him. Here are some of the biggest names in math, starting in ancient Egypt.

All is number

EUREKA!

AHMOSE about 1700 BC	**PYTHAGORAS** 569–475 BC	**EUCLID** 325–265 BC	**ARCHIMEDES** 287–212 BC

The world's first-known mathematician was an Egyptian called Ahmose. In 1700 BC he filled a 20-ft- (6-m-) long scroll of papyrus paper with 85 mathematical puzzles and their answers. One showed how to multiply by doubling repeatedly. It was a forerunner of the binary system that makes today's digital age possible. Ahmose was merely the person who copied the scroll—the true authors are lost in the past.

The Greek philosopher Pythagoras founded a secretive religion based on math. He said "all is number," believing math could explain anything. For instance, he showed that halving the length of a musical string gave a note one octave higher. Pythagoras realized Earth was round and proved the famous theorem about right-angled triangles. He also believed in reincarnation and forbade the eating of beans.

The Greek mathematician Euclid wrote the most successful math textbook ever: *The Elements*. It contained 250 years' worth of Greek math, all explained in simple and logical steps. *The Elements* was used to teach geometry in schools worldwide for more than 2,000 years, until recently. Euclid also proved there's an infinite number of prime numbers, and that the square root of 2 is an irrational number.

Archimedes is best known for leaping out of his bathtub and running naked down the street crying "Eureka!" after discovering the principle of hydrostatics. The most brilliant of all Greek mathematicians, he found pi to 3 decimal places, discovered the volume and surface area of a sphere, invented war machines, and explained pulleys and levers. He said, "Give me a lever long enough and a firm place to stand. I'll move the Earth."

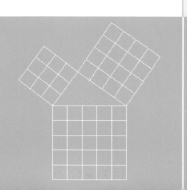

> "from these Indian numbers,
> 0 9 8 7 6 5 4 3 2 1,
> we derive great benefit"

> The universe is written in the language of mathematics

ERATOSTHENES 276–194 BC	AL KHWARIZMI 780–850 AD	FIBONACCI 1170–1250	GALILEO 1564–1642

The Greek scholar Eratosthenes was good not just at math but at astronomy, geography, and history, too. He devised a way of hunting for prime numbers, drew maps of the known world and the night sky, and figured out the need for leap years. But best of all, he worked out the size of Earth before most people knew it was round. His calculation led him to believe there must be a vast area of uncharted ocean—and he was right.

The Arab mathematician Al Khwarizmi lived in Baghdad. He wrote two books about math that helped spread Indian numbers and zero to the rest of the world. The terms "arithmetic" and "algorithm" both come from distortions of his name, and the word "algebra" comes from the title of his first book, *Ilm al-jabr wa'l muqabalah*. Also a geographer, he helped create a detailed map of the known world.

Leonardo da Pisa is best known by his nickname Fibonacci. The son of a traveling Italian merchant, he spent much of his life in Algeria, where the Arabs taught him how to use Indian numbers. Impressed by how these made arithmetic much easier, he wrote a book about them and so made them popular in Italy. He also discovered the Fibonacci series of numbers, which has links to nature and to the golden ratio.

Called the first true scientist, Galileo made telescopes and discovered Jupiter's moons, mountains on the Moon, and sunspots, which eventually blinded him. He also explored the force of gravity. He dropped balls off tall buildings but couldn't time them, so he rolled them down slopes instead. He showed they always increase speed in ratio with the square of the time taken. This helped Newton discover gravity.

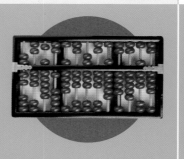

The machinery of the heavens is not like an animal but like a clock

I think, therefore I am

The more I see of men, the more I like my dog

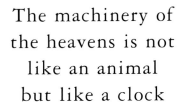

KEPLER 1571–1630	**DESCARTES** 1596–1650	**FERMAT** 1601–1665	**PASCAL** 1623–1662
The German astronomer Johann Kepler measured the paths of the planets before telescopes were invented and found that they orbited the Sun in ellipses, not circles. He showed that comets increase in speed as they near the Sun, and he found that a line drawn between the Sun and a planet will sweep over equal areas in equal times as the planet moves through its orbit.	René Descartes watched a fly while lying in bed and thought, "How can I explain the position of the fly at any moment?" He realized he could use three coordinates (x, y, and z) for each dimension of space (forward/back, up/down, left/right). Descartes was also the first person to use letters from the end of the alphabet to stand for values in algebra.	Pierre de Fermat created the most famous puzzle in math—"Fermat's last theorem." He wrote in the margin of a book that he had found a "truly marvelous proof" that the equation $x^n + y^n = z^n$ cannot be solved if n is more than 2, but said "there is not enough room to write it here." It took over 300 years to prove the theorem is true, but it seems likely that Fermat was lying.	A child prodigy, Pascal wrote a math book at age 16 and invented a calculating machine made of cogs and wheels when he was 19. He worked on gambling puzzles with Fermat and in doing so founded probability theory and uncovered the patterns in Pascal's triangle. At age 31 he became deeply religious and gave up math to spend his last years in prayer and meditation.

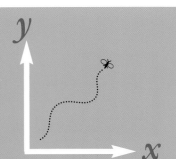

$$x^n + y^n = z^n$$

```
                    1
                  1   1
                1   2   1
              1   3   3   1
            1   4   6   4   1
          1   5  10  10   5   1
        1   6  15  20  15   6   1
      1   7  21  35  35  21   7   1
    1   8  28  56  70  56  28   8   1
  1   9  36  84 126 126  84  36   9   1
1  10  45 120 210 252 210 120  45  10   1
1  11  55 165 330 462 462 330 165  55  11   1
```

> I can calculate the motion of heavenly bodies but not the madness of people

> God does arithmetic

> If at first an idea is not absurd, then there is no hope for it

| **NEWTON** 1643–1727 | **EULER** 1707–1783 | **GAUSS** 1777–1855 | **EINSTEIN** 1879–1955 |

Inspired by Galileo's study of falling objects and Kepler's elliptical orbits, Isaac Newton worked out how gravity holds the universe together. He explained gravity like this. Throw a stone sideways and it falls to Earth. Throw it harder and it still falls. If you could throw it hard enough, it would keep going without falling— and that's precisely what the Moon is doing.

The Swiss mathematician Leonhard Euler ("oiler") was the most prolific mathematician ever. He wrote over 800 papers, many after he had gone blind in 1766. After he died it took 35 years to publish them all. He is most famous for solving the Königsberg Bridge puzzle, which was the start of network theory—without which today's microchips could not be made.

Classed as the third-greatest mathematician in history (after Archimedes and Newton), Karl Gauss was correcting his father's sums when he was 3. As a schoolboy he found an ingenious way of adding consecutive numbers quickly. Gauss also proved that any number is the product of primes, in one way only ($8 = 2 \times 2 \times 2$; $6 = 2 \times 3$; and so on).

Albert Einstein realized light moves at constant speed and is pulled by gravity. He also realized that mass and energy are versions of the same thing and devised an equation to show it (below). The equation shows that a tiny amount of mass (m) equals a vast amount of energy (E), since to make them equal you have to multiply the m by a very large number: the speed of light squared (c^2).

Gauss amused himself by *keeping records* of the lengths of famous men's lives—in days.

$$E = mc^2$$

ANSWERS

PAGE 26–27: BIG NUMBER QUIZ

1. Two. They're the ones you took!

2. Numbers for a front door.

3. Read the first sentence in the question again for the answer.

4. 100. Think about it…

5. Just over an hour.

6. Just the 4 dead crows. The rest flew away when they heard the gunshots.

7. 12 lb

8. Because 1 hour 20 minutes is the same as 80 minutes.

9. One

10. Three

11. One—the first one!

12. 63

13. There is no missing $1—it's a trick question. The question says "each customer ends up paying $9 and the waiter keeps $2, making $29," but the $2 should be subtracted from what the customers pay, not added.

14. There are two solutions. In the first solution, William and Arthur cross together first, taking 2 minutes, and William then returns with the flashlight, making 3 minutes in total. Charlie and Benedict cross next, taking 13 minutes in total so far. Arthur takes the light back (15 minutes) and then finally crosses with William (17 minutes). The second solution is nearly the same, but Arthur makes the first return with the light.

15. It's impossible, since four odd numbers will always add up to an even number.

16. The cowboy borrows his neighbor's horse, giving him a total of 12. He gives 6 horses to the oldest son, 3 horses to the middle son, and 2 horses to the youngest son. Then he gives the spare horse back to the neighbor.

17. Fill the 3-gallon pail and pour the water into the 5-gallon pail. This leaves a 2-gallon space in the top of the 5-gallon pail. Fill the 3-gallon pail again, and pour as much as possible into the 5-gallon pail to fill it. There's now 1 gallon of water left in the 3-gallon pail. Empty the 5-gallon pail, then pour the 1 gallon of water from the 3-gallon pail into it. Fill the 3-gallon pail once more and pour the water into the 5-gallon pail to make 4 gallons. Easy!

18. $64 \times 15625 = 1,000,000$. You can work this out by halving 1,000,000 six times.

19. Yes. This is how you do it:

Open and close first link:

⬯⬯ ⬯⬯⬯⬯⬯ ⬯⬯⬯

Open and close second link:

⬯ ⬯⬯⬯⬯⬯⬯⬯⬯

Open and close third link to create a circle.

20. Write the letter S to make "SIX."

21. 1113213211. If you read this out loud, it describes the line above in words: "One one, one three, two ones, three twos, one one."

22. 17 ostriches and 13 camels

PAGE 44–45: SQUARE AND TRIANGULAR NUMBERS

Prisoners' puzzle

Only prisoners in rooms with a square number on the door escape: 1, 4, 9, 16, 25, 36, and 49.

PAGE 46–47: PASCAL'S TRIANG

The road from A to B

There are 56 ways. The numbers form Pascal's triangle on its side.

PAGE 54–55: SHAPES WITH 4 SIDE

1.

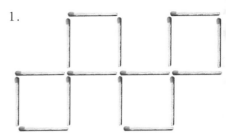

2.

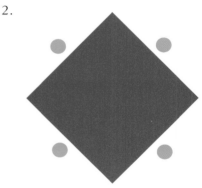

3. 14. The diagonal line is the sar length as the radius of the circle (7 + 7).

4.

5. The journey takes as long as it would take to go to C if there was no wind: 30 minutes. This is how pilots actually plan their trips.

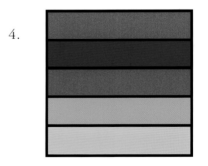

PAGE 58–59: THE THIRD DIMENSION

	FACES	EDGES	CORNERS
CUBE	6	12	8
TETRAHEDRON	4	6	4
OCTAHEDRON	8	12	6
DODECAHEDRON	12	30	20
ICOSAHEDRON	20	30	12

Number of faces + number of corners = number of edges + 2

PAGE 60–61: SOCCER BALLS AND BUCKYBALLS

Cube puzzle

You need six cuts, since the central cube has six faces.

PAGE 62–63: ROUND AND ROUND

Rolling coins

Most people think the coin will make a half-turn, but in fact it makes a complete turn.

The bear hunter

White. The hunter must be at the North Pole, so it's a polar bear.

Flying tonight

The pilot must have been flying to exactly the other side of the world from the airport. Wherever the girl was going, he could fly past her destination.

The area of the pink band

They're the same area. The radius of the circles increases by 1 unit each time. The area of the three middle rings, therefore, is $\pi 3^2$, or 9π. The area of the blue ring = $\pi 5^2 - \pi 4^2$, which is also 9π.

PAGE 66–67: SHAPES THAT STRETCH

Topological shapes

The doughnut is equivalent to the needle, thread spool, cup, and funnel. The rugby ball is equivalent to the glass, soccer ball, battery, die, and pencil. The wrench is equivalent to the scissors and bowl. The brick is the odd one out.

The Möbius strip

When you cut along the center, the Möbius strip turns into one band twice as long. When you cut a third of the way from the edge, the strip turns into two rings linked together.

The two ribbons

A square

Monk-y puzzle

Yes. Imagine two people walking up and down the mountain the same day. Whatever their speed, they must meet each other at some point.

PAGE 68–69: MIRROR MIRROR

Axes of symmetry

Tape: infinite (or 4 if you think the plastic struts matter). Flower: about as many as the number of petals. Star: 5. Bat: 1. Scissors: 1. Crab: 0. Coin: 7. Spoon: 1.

PAGE 70–71: AMAZING MAZES

Big maze

Dice maze

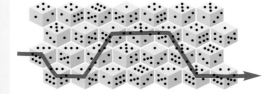

Spiral maze

All the dots are outside the maze. To find out whether a dot is inside or outside, count the number of lines between the dot and outer edge of the maze. An even number means the dot is outside; an odd number means the dot is inside.

Colored sticks

Blue, red, pink, pale blue, yellow, pale green, gray, dark green.

Twelve connected circles

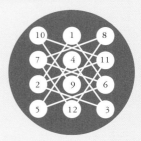

Königsberg bridges

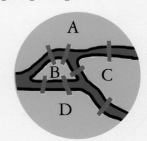

The Swiss mathematician Leonhard Euler used network theory to solve this famous puzzle in 1736. Imagine the town as having four regions: A, B, C, and D. On your walk through town, you'd walk in and out of at least two of these regions the same number of times, so they'd have to have an even number of bridges. But all the regions have an odd number of bridges, so the walk must be impossible.

PAGE 72–73: PUZZLING SHAPES

1. Most people think the answer is 32, since it seems to double each time. In fact, it's 31.

2. All the letters above the division are made of straight lines, while all the letters below contain curves.

3.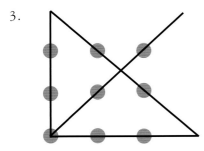

4. By making two vertical cuts at right angles and one horizontal cut right through the cake.

5. First make a horizontal cut, as though you're slicing open a bagel. Then make a vertical cut to slice the circle into two semicircles. Finally, stack one on top of the other and make a cut like this:

6. Poke your finger through the handle and give it a push!!!

7.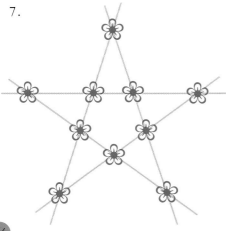

8.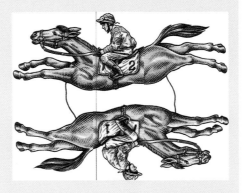

9. The ant can walk around the octahedron but not the cube or the tetrahedron. The journey is impossible if more than two corners of a shape have an *odd number* of connections to other corners. For a similar puzzle, see the Königsberg bridges, page 71.

10. There are 24 ways of solving the sliding coin puzzle. Here's one:

11. Green.

12.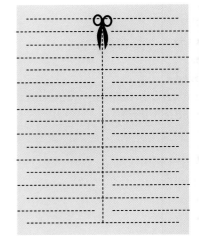

PAGE 82–83: LOGIC

Chessboard

It's impossible to cover all the squares with dominoes. Each domino must lie on both a black and a white square, so the dominoes will cover an equal number of each. But since the missing squares are both black, there will be two spare white squares that can't be covered.

Who shaves the barber?

Nobody—she doesn't shave!

The prisoner

The prisoner can't know which day the hanging will take place o Therefore, he can't be hung on the last day, because he'd know the da before. Likewise, he can't be hung the day before last, because he'd know the day before that. Workin backward, the same thing applies to every day, so the prisoner can't be hung at all!

The tiger

If the woman says "you will let the child go," the tiger can do

what he wants. It would be better
if she says "you will eat the
child," but then the situation is
a paradox—the tiger can neither
eat the child (because the
prediction would be correct)
nor let the child go (because the
prediction would be incorrect).

Three doors

If you don't change your mind,
you have a one-third chance of
winning the car. If you do change
your mind, your have a two-
thirds chance of winning. Many
people find this answer very hard
to believe, but it's true. For
an explanation, go here:
www.jimloy.com/puzz/monty.htm

Three hats

Black. A could only know her
hat color if both B and C were
wearing white (since not all three
hats are white), but she answers
"No." That means there must be
a black hat on at least one of the
others. B realizes this and looks
at C to see if her hat is white,
which would mean B's was the
black one. But it isn't, so B
answers "No." That means C
must have the black hat. C
knows this because she heard
the other sisters' answers.

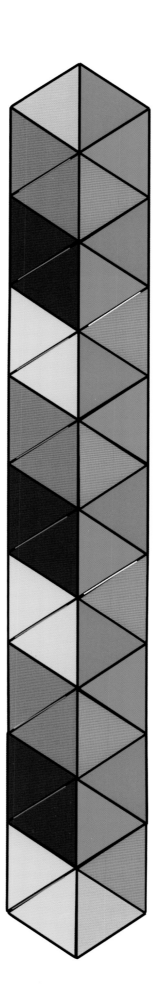

MAKE A HEXAFLEXAGON

1. Copy this pattern and color
in as shown. Better still, make
an enlarged color photocopy or
scan into a computer and print
it out as large as possible.
2. Fold in half along the
middle so the triangles
are on the outside.
3. Glue the two halves to each
other to form a long strip with
triangles on both sides. Let
the glue dry completely.
4. Hold it so the side with
yellow stripes is on top. Fold
along each green line, with the
green lines in the troughs of
the folds, so that triangles of
the same color come face-to-
face. The strip should form
a flattened coil.
5. Now fold along each white
line, with the white lines on
the peaks of the folds, to make
a hexagon. One side will be
entirely green. The other side
will be mostly pink, except
for the last, unfolded triangle.
6. Fold over the last triangle
and glue the gray faces
together. Let the glue dry.
7. To flex the hexaflexagon,
pinch two corners at once to
form a 3-sided star, then open
it out like a flower. Each time
you do this, it will change
color completely. See if you
can make all 6 colors appear.

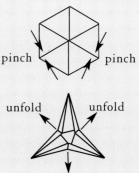

INDEX

Acknowledgments

Dorling Kindersley would like to thank the following people for help with this book: Jacqueline Gooden, Elizabeth Haldane, Tory Gordon-Harris, Janice Hawkins, Robin Hunter, Anthony Limerick, Laura Roberts. DK would also like to thank the following for permission to reproduce their images (key: a=above, b=below, c=center, l=left, r=right, t=top):

Alamy Images: AA World Travel Library 50c, 53br; Andrew Woodley 28-29, 35b; Che Garman 33bcr, 74-75, 76bcr1, 76bcr2, 76bcr3, 76bcr4, 76bcr5, 76br1, 76br2, 76br3, 76br4, 76br5; TNT Magazine 78bl. Ancient Art & Architecture Collection: 46tr, 89cla. The Art Archive: Institut de France Paris/Dagli Orti 83tc. Johnny Ball: 47tr. www.bridgeman.co.uk: National Gallery, London, UK 85cla; Pinacoteca di Brera, Milan, Italy 84car. Corbis: 88bl; Alinari Archives 88cal; Archivo Iconografico, S.A. 89clb, 89car, 90cal; Bettmann

32tl, 44cfl, 88car, 89cra, 90cla, 90cla, 90car, 91cra, 91cla, 91car; Carl & Ann Purcell 79cfr; David Reed 57crb; Duomo/Chris Trotman 9cra; Gianni Dagli Orti 5tl, 6clb, 14-15; Hulton-Deutsch Collection 88cra; Jim Reed 74t, 78car; Jon Feingersh 52tl, 52cra, 52crb, 52crb, 52bl, 52bcl, 52car, 52tcl; Joyce Choo 44-45; Keren Su 11cfr; Lee Snider/Photo Imag 52br, 60-61; Leonard de Selva 91cla; M. Angelo 18clb, 18b 19crb; Matthias Kulka 36-37 65br; Patrick Darby 36cla; The State Hermitage Museum St Petersburg, Russia 67c; Reuters 8bl, 8-9, 22br, 27cfl, 38bl, 62clb, 74-75, 78-79, 89bl; Rob Matheson 77cbr; Staffan Widstrand 16tr; Stefano Bianchetti 61br, 90cra. DK Images: Alan Hill & Barbara Winter/British Museum 6ca, 6cal, 6car, 14clb, 14cbl, 14clb2; Andy Crawford/David Roberts 45br British Museum 6-7, 18-19b; Colin Keates/Natural History Museum, London 50-51, 57cal, 68-69, 77cbr; Dave King/Science Museum, Londo 6cbr; David Jordan/The Ivy Press Limited 6-7, 10cr, 11cl 12bl, 13bl, 13bcl, 42bl, 42bc 42br, 43bl, 43bc, 43br; Geof Brightling/South of England Rare Breeds Centre, Ashford, Kent 27cfr; Guy Ryecart/The Ivy Press Limited 5bl, 74clb, 76cb; Jerry Young 83br; Judi Miller/Keller & Ross 64c; Michel Zabe/Conaculta-Inah-Mex/Instituto Nacional de Antropologia e Historia. 18-19t; Museum of London 86-8 Philip Dowell 14tr, 14cra; T Sean Hunter Collection 89br; Tina Chambers/National Maritime Museum, London 65bcr, 82c. Janice Hawkins: 16-17. The M.C. Escher Company, Holland: 84br, 84l 85bl, 85bcr. Getty Images: Altrendo 28cla, 33cl; Botani 74cl, 80cr; FoodPix 39cfl; Robert Harding World Imagery 50tl, 70-71. Magic Eye Inc. www.magiceye.com: 85cra. NASA: 63br, 81cl. National Geographic Image Collection: Jonathan Blair 33bcl. Photolibrary.com: Hagiwara Brian 5cla, 33br; Morrison Ted 33bl. Powerstock: age fotostock 79br. Science Photo Library: Alfred Pasieka 80cl, 80c; J. Bernholc Et Al, North Caroli State University 60cl; John Durham 57c; Kenneth Libbrecht 57cb; M-Sat Ltd 81c; Pekka Parviainen 81cr; Susumu Nishinaga 57cfr. Spaarnestad Fotoarchief: 6cal 12tl, 12tc, 12tr, 13tl, 13tc, 13tr. Topfoto.co.uk: Silvio Fiore 88cla.

All other images © Dorling Kindersley.